Philetus Theodore Pockman, Jeremiah F. Yates

History of the Reformed Church

East Greenbush, Rensselaer County, New York

Philetus Theodore Pockman, Jeremiah F. Yates

History of the Reformed Church
East Greenbush, Rensselaer County, New York

ISBN/EAN: 9783337296230

Printed in Europe, USA, Canada, Australia, Japan

Cover: Foto ©Lupo / pixelio.de

More available books at **www.hansebooks.com**

"ERECTED A. D. 1860.
A. BIRCH, Builder."

HISTORY

OF THE

REFORMED CHURCH,

AT

East Greenbush,

Rensselaer County, New York.

"One generation shall praise thy works to another."

COMPILED BY
REV. P. THEO. POCKMAN, A. M.

PUBLISHED 1891.

J. HEIDINGSFELD, Printer, New Brunswick, N. J.

INTRODUCTORY.

THE little hair-trunk, tender with age, has poured out its contents at our feet. On the seared and yellow leaves were written deeds, bills, receipts, etc., which told plainly enough that this was the treasurer's chest. It has long and faithfully preserved these, together with the "collector's" books. It has many a quiet tale to relate of early struggle and devotion to the temporal interests of Zion.

From different hands there have come to us the various records of our Mother Church, telling their individual stories of how God hath wrought among the people for over a hundred years. Some of these are in a foreign language, for our forefathers were *Dutch*, but all are in a good state of preservation.

These pages have been scanned with keen interest, and such items noted here and there as may be of general interest to the reader. It is worthy of special mention that we have been enabled to make out a complete list of all who have served in the Consistory from the beginning, and also that we can present a full catalogue of members.

The records of *births* and *baptisms* are in a good state of preservation, but will not be found transcribed in these pages. Baptisms began in January, 1788.

The record of marriages is complete from October 5th, 1788, when Henry Shebley and Elizabeth Shans were married; also Wynanot Van De Bergh and Eva Witbeck: Rev. J. V. C. Romeyn performing the ceremony.

The first thought of this modest volume was awakened four years ago, when the church observed her centennial, and much of the contents were collected at that time by the persevering labors of the historian, Rev. Jeremiah F. Yates, of Fort Edward, N. Y., who has most generously put everything into the hands of the compiler.

In the hope that these pages will keep alive the interest of generations yet unborn in the church of our fathers, and that the name of the Great Head of the Church will be glorified in some measure through them, they are now scattered broadcast.

"Church of my sires—my love to thee
Was nurtured in my infancy,
And now maturer thoughts approve
The object of that infant love.
Linked to my soul with hooks of steel,
By all I say, and do, and feel—
By records that refresh my eye,
In the rich page of memory—
By blessings at thine altars given—
By scenes which lift the soul to Heaven;
By monuments that humbly rise
Memorials of the good and wise—
By graves forever sad and dear,
Still reeking with my constant tear;
Where those in honored slumber lie,
Whose deaths have taught me how to die.
And shall I not with all my powers,
Watch round thy venerable towers?
And can I bid the pilgrim flee,
To holier refuge than to thee?"

LOCALITY.

THE original deed of sale for the land forming the Van Rensselaer Manor (a tract 24 by 48 miles), lying about Albany, then Fort Orange, was seen by Gen. James Grant Wilson at Amsterdam a few years ago. It is dated August 13th, 1630, and is full of Indian names. Gen. Wilson has a photograph of the paper. This is supposed to be the oldest record of the kind pertaining to New York State lands.

The deed of sale for Manhattan Island was long ago lost or destroyed.—*Albany Journal, Oct.* 29, 1889.

The names of Van Buren, Van Hegen, Staats, Witbeck and Bris were found in the township as early as 1630. Van Denburgh, Cuyler and Van Wesipe were also among the earliest families in the old township of Greenbush.

A Mr. Van Buren occupied a brick house on the river road, about three miles south of the village of Greenbush, which was erected over one hundred years ago, and stands on a stone foundation that was laid in 1630. The original house was a stone structure, but its walls became so damp that it was taken down.

The oldest dwelling in the valley of the Hudson, and one of the most ancient in this part of the country, is situated just five miles south of Albany, upon the east side of the river. The old Staats stone mansion, or fort, dates far back, even to the remotest history of our Colonial days. No doubt when the Mayflower was tempest-tossed upon the angry billows of the Atlantic, and but a few years after the first trading post was established by the Dutch, which was the origin of the Capital city of New York, this little stone fort, with its thick and substantial walls, stood the ravages of time, as the rugged oak of the forest stands, defying the tempest's fury or the wintry blast. The Staats mansion was standing long ere Queen Anne ruled over the British Possessions, and was more than a century old at the time of Gen. Washington's birth. It is built of stone and brick. The stone portion of the building is the first or original house; the other portion is a comparatively modern structure.

The Staats family have occupied the same homestead and farm all these years. The present generation is the *seventh* from the original proprietor.

(C. Van Rensselaer, Hudson, N. Y.)

Another dwelling in the township contests the claim of priority and speaks of early life in the vicinity. In the suburbs of Greenbush village to the south is found an ancient structure, which was built at the time Holland held sway. Its front walls facing the river, are pierced with two portholes. It originally had more in the different walls of the building. This house was erected by Hendrick Van Rensselaer about 1642. It is commonly known as the old Manor House.

(C. Van Rensselaer.)

Among the memorial tablets erected in Albany and vicinity during Bi-Centennial year (1886) is one placed in the walls of this Van Rensselaer house bearing this inscription:

"Supposed to be the oldest building in the United States and to have been erected in 1642 as a manor house and place of defence known as Fort Cralo, General Abercrombie's headquarters while marching to attack Fort Ticonderoga in 1758, where it is said that at the cantonment east of the house near the old well, the army surgeon, Dr. Shamburg, composed the popular song, 'Yankee Doodle.'"

The early settlement of the township is no more surely authenticated than is the establishment of religious worship.

A marble slab in the vestibule of the church relates the fact year after year—"Built 1786"—which was the year previous to the organization of the society as a Christian church.

The deed for the land upon which the church was built was given to the Consistory by Stephen Van Rensselaer, Esq., on April 8th, 1793, and reads as follows:

Stephen Van Rensselaer, Esq.,
         to
The Minister, Elders and Deacons of the } Release.
Reformed Protestant Low Dutch Church
in Greenbush.

"This Indenture, made the Eighth day of April in the year of our Lord one thousand seven hundred and ninety-three, Between Stephen Van Rensselaer, Esq., Lord and Proprietor of the Manor of Rensselaerwyck, in the Counties of Albany and Rensselaer, of the first part, and Jacobus Van Campe Romeyn, *Minister*, Christopher Yates, John E. Van Alen, Stephen Muller and Huybert Ostrander, *Elders*, and Barent Van Denbergh, John Lewis, Thomas Mesick and Jonathan Ostrander, *Deacons*, Trustees of the Reformed Protestant Low Dutch Church of Greenbush, of the second part: Witnesseth, that the said Stephen Van Rensselaer, for and in consideration of promoting the Christian Religion, and for advancing the Interest of the said Church, as for and in consideration of the Sum of ten Shillings, lawful money of the State of New York, to him in hand paid by the said party of the second part, at and before the Ensealing and Delivery hereof, the Receipt whereof he doth hereby acknowledge, Hath given, Granted, Remised, Released and Confirmed, and by these presents Doth give, grant, Remise, Release and Confirm unto the said Jacobus Van Campe Romeyn, *Minister*, Christopher Yates, John E. Van Alen, Stephen Muller and Huybert Ostrander, *Elders*, and Barent Van Denbergh, John Lewis, Thomas Mesick and Jonathan Ostrander, *Deacons*, trustees of the said Church in their actual Possession now being, and to their Successors forever: All that certain piece or Parcel of Glebe Land situate, lying and being in Greenbush, in the County of Rensselaer, and Manor aforesaid, whereon the Church Now stands, and is bounded as follows, to wit: Beginning at a point which is distant one chain forty-seven links from the Northeast Corner of said Church, on a Course North twenty-seven degrees East and runs thence North thirty-three degrees

West two chains ninety-six links, then North fifty-seven degrees East five chains, then South thirty-three degrees East five chains, then South fifty-seven degrees West five chains, then South thirty-three degrees East two chains ninety-six links, then South fifty-seven degrees West four chains, then North thirty-three degrees West five chains, then North fifty-seven degrees East four chains, to the place of beginning, Containing four Acres and five-tenths of an Acre; TOGETHER with all and singular the Hereditaments and appurtenances thereunto belonging, or in anywise appertaining, and the Reversion and Reversions, Remainder and Remainders, Rents, Issues and profits thereof, and of every part thereof, with the appurtenances; To HAVE AND TO HOLD the said piece or parcel of Glebe land and premises unto them the said Jacobus Van Campe Romeyn, *Minister*, Christopher Yates, John E. Van Alen, Stephen Muller and Huybert Ostrander, *Elders*, and Barent Van Denbergh, John Lewis, Thomas Mesick and Jonathan Ostrander, *Deacons*, trustees as aforesaid, and to their Successors forever, to and for the Sole and only proper use, benefit and behoof of the said Reformed protestant low Dutch Church of Greenbush, and for no other use or purpose whatsoever; Provided ALWAYS, and these presents are upon this Express Condition, that, whenever it shall so happen that the Divine Service shall cease to be performed by the Congregation in the Church aforesaid, or that they shall otherwise be unable to support a Minister for the Service, that then it shall and may be lawful for the said Stephen Van Rensselaer, his heirs and Assigns, into the premises aforesaid to Re-enter, and the same to have again, Repossess and Enjoy, anything herein to the Contrary Notwithstanding. In Witness whereof the parties to these presents have hereunto Interchangeably set their hands and Seals the Day and Year above written.

STEPHEN VAN RENSSELAER."

" STATE OF NEW YORK, *ss*.

This twelfth day of August, one thousand eight hundred and

nine, personally appeared before me the within named Stephen Van Rensselaer, to me known to be the same person described in and who executed the within Indenture of Release and acknowledged to have executed the same. I therefore allow it to be Recorded.   T. HANSEN, Master in Chancery."

"Recorded 3d October at 6 o'clock P. M. in Book of Deeds No. 6, page 22, Clerk's Office, Rensselaer County.

Examined by me.   R. M. LIVINGSTON,
Fees, $1.20.   Dep'y Cl'k."

"Sealed and Delivered in the presence of
WM. GROSON,
SCHUYLER SWITS."

CHURCH BUILDINGS.

The first church edifice was erected in 1786. It was built of wood, forty or forty-five feet square, with gambrel roof running north and south, and with the entrance on the east side. There were six windows on a side, three above the gallery and three below it. The entrance to the gallery was by stairs on the *outside*, beginning at the southeast corner and running up on the south side. It was painted *yellow*. Mr. William Snook says it was for many years known as "The old yellow church." Services on Sabbath, according to his earliest recollection, were two, forenoon and afternoon, and only one hour apart, the people tying their horses in the rear of the church and eating their lunch there, while their teams fed on hay, which they had brought with them. Mr. Snook also says that he often heard his father say that he drew the *second* stick of timber for the first church—a Mr. Van Rensselaer living near the river having drawn the first stick.

Revs. Romeyn, Zabriskie, Labagh, Marselus, Taylor and Dumont preached in this building before any alterations were made in the structure.

Second building. The marble slab that gives the date of the first edifice—"1786"—also records the date of the first alteration, which practically made the church another building, viz.—"Enlarged 1829." In October of that year the following changes were ordered: An addition of thirteen feet to be made to whole front (east) to contain one large door, and two flights of stairs on the inside to the gallery. The roof to be turned gable end to the road, so as to run east and west. Two doors to enter the body of the church; one opposite each side aisle. Two recesses for stoves at front end. Windows then in front to be closed and inserted in the new part. Two windows on the north side and two windows on the south side in the new part of the building, and a door in front of the middle aisle. The south door leading to the gallery to be closed.

A porch in front of the large door, and an arched window over the door. A *cupola* at the east end twenty feet above the eaves.

The following agreement was recently found among the papers of the Rev. John A. Liddell. It refers to changes made in the rear of the church in 1833 :

"Memorandum of agreement made and entered into by and between Henry Vandenbergh, Jno. Link, Barent Hoes, Jno. Breese, James Elliott and Richard Waring, of the first part, and Jno. G. Rorabeck of the second part. Whereas the said Rorabeck is to erect or build an addition to the Prot. Ref Dutch Church in the town of Greenbush (of which the Rev. J. A. Liddell is pastor)—Said addition is to be placed on the west end of said church, to extend West fifteen feet from the said Church and North and South width and height of the old church to be built in a good substantial and workmanlike manner and in all things to correspond with the old Church inside and out, except the frame of the roof, which is to be supported with purline plates in a sufficient manner to support the sealing and roof, and one post to extend from (which will be) the centre post, under the north and south Galleries to the sealing of the said church to correspond with the posts now under the Gallery. The pulpit to be placed at the west end of said Church with a flight of stairs on each side up to the entrance thereof, Railing and Bannisters to be of black walnut, a perpendicular schrale on said railing neatly finished—a closet under each flight of stairs with doors, locks and keys to the same. One slip less on each side of the Pulpit to leave room for the steps to the Pulpit. With a good stone wall under the new part of the church, two feet thick, three feet from the bottom of the sill downward, with good stone Butments of the same depth and two feet square of flat stones under the floor foundation, and under the posts that support the Gallery. The plastering to be of two coats and good quality to correspond with that of the old part of the church, and white washed. The windows in the new part of the church to be checked. The slips to be made to correspond with them in the old part of said Church, fashioned and finished corresponding with the old ones. The whole of the new part to be fashioned and finished to correspond with the old part inside and out, to have two coats of paint to match those now on said Church. Said Rorabeck is to have the materials taken from the west end of the church, and use so much thereof in the erection of the addition to said Church as may be good and sufficient.

In consideration of the said Rorabeck's faithful performance on his part the said Vandenbergh, Links, Hoes, Breese, Elliott, and Waring agree and promise to pay the said Rorabeck five hundred and sixty-five Dollars in manner following.

At the time of commencing said building Two hundred Dollars $200, when said building is enclosed Two hundred Dollars, and when the said building is completed to the satisfaction of the said party of the first part one hundred and sixty-five Dollars. The whole sum $565.

The said Rorabeck is to have the addition to said Church finished on or before the thirtieth day of October, one Thousand eight hundred and Thirty Three.

In witness whereof the parties to these presents have hereunto set their hands and affixed their seals this   day of   one thousand eight hundred and thirty-three."

These alterations changed the appearance and capacity of the house and formed the second structure.

The present handsome and substantial structure was erected in 1860, on nearly the same site, only changing the foundation sufficiently to make the building parallel with the highway. The corner-stone was laid June 5th, 1860, at the northeast corner. It is 72 feet long by 50 feet wide and 35 feet high, with organ loft and gallery across the front end only. It is of brick with brown stone water tables, etc. The church was without a pastor during its erection. It was dedicated April, 1861. Rev. Dr. E. P. Rogers, of the First Reformed Church of Albany, officiated. His predecessor in that church, Rev. Eilardus Westerlo, performed a similar service for the *first* edifice seventy-four years before.

PARSONAGES.

The first house used as a parsonage was in the township of Schodack. The Schodack congregation provided this for the minister. Rev. Mr. Romeyn lived in this house.

The second parsonage was at Blooming Grove, on the line dividing the two congregations of Greenbush and Wynantskill. It appears that the Rev. Mr. Romeyn bought this house at first and sold it to the two congregations for a parsonage, after his successor arrived. In 1802 it was bought by the church for 150 pounds, and fully paid for in 1805. The last installment of this sum was "transmitted to Mr. Romeyn by Capt. Boyd, of Albany, who brought up our Bond, which was cancelled."

The following "Quit Claim Deed" has been found, but the transaction seems not to be recorded in the church records :

THIS INDENTURE, made the tenth day of January in the year of our Lord one thousand eight hundred and three, BETWEEN Peter D. VanDyck, of the town of Greenbush, in the county of Rensselaer, and Margaret VanDyck, his wife, of the first part, and the minister, elders and deacons of the Reformed Protestant Dutch Church of Greenbush, in the county of Albany, their successors of the second part,

WITNESSETH, That the said parties, of the first part, for and in consideration of the sum of three hundred and fifty pounds, lawful money of New York, to them in hand paid, by the said parties, of the second part, the receipt whereof is hereby confessed and acknowledged; HAVE bargained, sold, remised and quit-claimed; and by these presents Do bargain, sell, remise and forever QUITCLAIM, unto the said parties, of the second part, and to their successors forever, the one equal moiety or half of all that that certain lot of ground situate, lying and being in the town of Greenbush, in the county of Rensselaer, with all the buildings and improvements on the same, butted and bounded as follows, to wit : Beginning at the corner post of the Court-yard fence, which is distant two chains and thirteen links on a course south, sixty-four degrees west from the southwest corner of the dwelling house of the said Peter D. Van Dyck, and running thence south seventy-five degrees and ten minutes, east nine chains and ninety links to a stake and stones, then south thirty degrees, west one chain and sixteen links to a stake and stones, then south fifty-five degrees, east fifteen chains and ninety-six links, then north twenty-nine degrees fifteen minutes, east six chains forty-four links to the south line of the farm of David M. De Foreest, then along the same north fifty-six degrees fifteen minutes, west six chains thirty links, then south seventy-nine degrees, west forty-six links, then north fifty-one degrees, west nine chains forty-one links, then south twenty-nine degrees fifteen minutes, west three chains sixty-six links, then north sixty-three degrees, west eleven chains ten links, and then south eight degrees, west four chains fifteen links to the place of beginning, containing thirteen acres of land,

TOGETHER with all and singular the hereditaments and appurtenances thereunto belonging, or in any wise appertaining, and the reversion and reversions, remainder and remainders, rents, issues and profits thereof; and all the estate, right, title, interest, claim or demand whatsoever, of the said parties of the first part, either in law or equity, of, in and to the above bargained premises, with the hereditaments and appurtenances. To HAVE AND TO HOLD, the said premises, above described, with the appurtenances to the said parties of the second part, and to their successors, to the sole and only proper use, benefit and behoof of the said parties of the second part, their successors forever.

IN WITNESS whereof, *the parties to these presents, have hereunto interchangeably set their hands and seals, the day and year first above written.*   PETER D. VAN DYCK,
            MARGARET VAN DYCK.

Sealed and delivered, }
  in presence of   }

The *heirs and assigns* being obliterated in the eight line, and the word *successors* being inserted in place thereof, and the word *all* in the same line being also obliterated; *heirs and assigns* being obliterated in the twenty-fourth and twenty-fifth lines and the word *successors* interlined in both places instead thereof.
      LEONARD GANSEVOORT, JUNR.,
      ANN BEEKMAN.

Be it remembered that on the tenth day of January, in the year of our Lord one thousand eight hundred and three, personally appeared before me, Leonard Gansevoort, Junr., one of the judges of the Court of Common Pleas of the county of Rensselaer, Peter D. Van Dyck and Margaret, his wife, both to me personally known, who severally acknowledged that they had signed, sealed and as their voluntary act and deed delivered the within indenture for the uses and purposes theirein mentioned, and the said Margaret Van Dyck, being by me examined privately, apart from her husband, the said Peter D. Van Dyck, acknowledged that she executed the same without any fear or compulsion of her said husband, and I, having examined the same and finding therein no erasures or interlineation other than those noted, do allow the same to be recorded.

LEONARD GANSEVOORT, Junr.

Recorded this Eighteenth day of February, 1803, in Book No. 3 of Deeds, Page 225 & 6, in the Clerk's office in the County of Rensselaer. N. SCHUYLER, Cl'k.

About 1807 "Ten acres of land adjoining the parsonage" were purchased by the Church, Dominie Zabriskie advancing some of the money on it.

In 1815 the Greenbush Church sold the parsonage at Blooming Grove, "one-third consideration money to go to Blooming Grove."

Revs. Zabriskie and Labagh lived at Blooming Grove.

On October 19, 1815, the Consistory decided to buy the property of Charles Doughty.

This is probably the property owned for some time by William Barringer, and afterwards by Michael Warner, and now owned by Mr. Crandall.

The following survey of the parsonage and Green lots, made in 1825, is preserved.

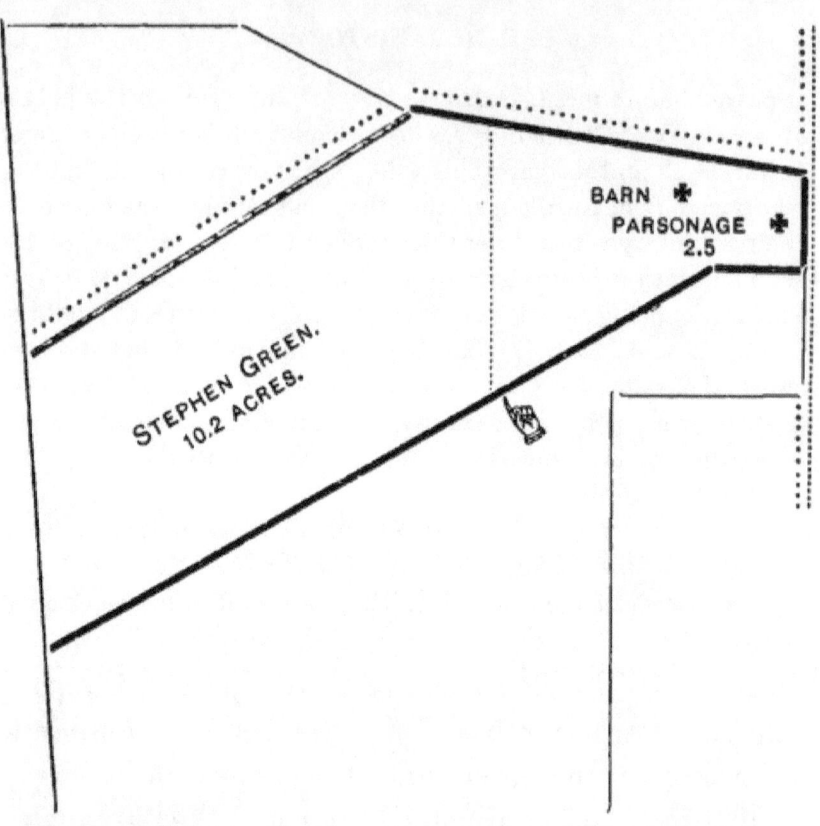

The heavy lines on the above map represent the parsonage and lands thereto attached, belonging to the Consistory of the Church of Greenbush, a part of which they have lately sold to Stephen Green as represented by the dotted line and which will be described as follows:

Beginning at a stake and stones standing in the south line of the said lot and at the distance of 5.85 on a course S, 41 degrees W. from the S. W. corner of the barn on the said parsonage and runs from the said stake and stones.

1. N. 3 degrees 5 minutes, E 6.25 to a stake in the north line and in the south side of the road, then along the same
2. N. 73 degrees 30 minutes 1.00 to a stake, then
3. N. 85 minutes, W. 3.88, then
4. S. 52 degrees 30 minutes, W. 11.80 to a stake in the west line, then
5. S. 9 degrees, E. 1.22 to a stake, then
6. S. 5 degrees 45 minutes, E. 4.74 to a stake and stones, and then
7. N. 64 degrees, E. 14.46 to the place of beginning; contents, 10.2 acres.

Returned 12th August, 1825, by
      EVERT VAN ALEN, Surveyor.

Revs. Marselus, Taylor and Dumont lived here, and probably Liddell in the early part of his ministry.

What is now familiarly known as the old parsonage was built in 1831 on land belonging to the church. On April 15, 1831, a committee was appointed to get subscriptions, and to select a site for a parsonage "between the church and Esquire James Lansings's house."

In the spring of 1835 a wing was added to the north side of the parsonage at a cost of $258. Messrs. Perkins and Carpenter were the builders. The *well* was dug the same year. On Dec. 1, 1835, the Consistory adopted these resolutions relative to the well:

Resolved, That any person wishing water from the pump in the Dutch Church parsonage yard shall after the first of May next (1836) pay the sum of two dollars in advance, each and every year during the time they shall use it, except in certain cases where the Consistory think proper to commute.

Carried by a large majority.

Resolved, That no person shall have the privilege of bringing any animal into the yard for the purpose of watering the same.

Wells were an expensive luxury in those days!

This house was occupied by Revs. Liddell, Stimson, Talmage and Anderson. During Mr. Wilson's pastorate it was rented, he always boarding at other places.

The old parsonage was sold to Miles Traver on Jan. 18, 1873, for $2,025.

The new parsonage was built in the year 1872. On the 26th of March of that year the Consistory decided to build a new parsonage and sell the old one.

The Building Committee was composed of Jacob Kimmey, John N. Pockman, Andrew Tweedale, Isaac Hays and Jacob M. Cotton.

On the 20th of April, 1873, this committee reported the parsonage completed at a cost of $5,665.67. This beautiful house with its capacious grounds added very much to the comfort of the minister's family.

On July 7, 1873, the above committee was instructed to have a well dug at the new parsonage at a cost of $150. A suitable barn was also erected; and all these were located on the middle portion of the Breese lot—that comprised the plot of ground purchased on Dec. 26, 1866, by the Church of Miss Berthia L. Staats for the sum of $3,000. The warranty deed was given April 10, 1867. The north lot was disposed of to the Misses Yates and the south lot became the property of John N. Pockman.

No more desirable place could be found in the village for a pastor's residence.

GLEBE LOTS.

On March 8th, 1798, it was determined to lease the Glebe Lots belonging to the church, that they might become a source of profit to the church.

An annual rent of not less than three pounds was to be reserved on each lot.

Monday, the nineteenth of March, 1798, at ten o'clock A. M., was fixed upon as the time of sale. Upon that date the following sales were effected:

Lot No. 1, purchased by Gerardus Beekman, for £1.15.0.

Lot No. 2, purchased by John Brees, for £2.8.0.

Lot No. 3, purchased by Gerrit Brees, for £2.2.0.

Lot No. 4, purchased by Henry K. Van Rensselaer, for £2.18.0.

Lot No. 5, purchased by Gerrit O. Lansingh, for £4.0.0.

The above purchase money became due on May 1st, 1798, when the leases were executed to the purchasers. Previous to this date a *Seal* was to be procured pertaining to the body corporate of the church, and it was left to the discretion of the minister to *direct the device*.

On March 4th, 1809, three lots of ground were conveyed to Dr. John S. Miller, lying north of the lot in possession of Manassah Knowlton, reserving a yearly rent on said lots of three pounds.

The accompanying survey is undoubtedly of the lot now owned by Samuel S. Warner:

Beginning at a stake and stones standing on the south line of the Parsonage lot and at the distance of 5.85 on a course forty-one degrees west from the southwest corner of the barn on the said parsonage lot, and runs from said stake and stones north three degrees fifteen minutes east, 6.25, to a stake on the north line and on the south side of the road; then along the same easterly to the Rensselaer and Columbia turnpike road; then along the same southerly to the northeast corner of William P. Morrison's farm; then westerly along the north line of said farm to the place of beginning, containing 2.5 acres of land.

DEEDS IN TRUST.

THIS INDENTURE, made this tenth day of June, one thousand eight hundred and fifty-seven, BETWEEN Cornelius Van Rensselaer and Maria L., his wife, of the town of Clinton in the county of Rensselaer and State of New York, parties of the first part, and Nathaniel S. Payne, Simeon Ostrander, Joseph S. Hare, Charles Rhoda, John Pockman, Henry Salisbury, John Gilbert and William Link, The Consistory of the Reformed Dutch Church of Greenbush (now the town of Clinton) and their successors in office, in trust for all the heirs of Col. Nicholas Van Rensselaer, late of the town of Greenbush, deceased, of the second part,

WITNESSETH, That the said parties of the first part, for and in consideration of FIVE dollars, to them duly paid by the said parties of the second part, have bargained, sold, remised and quit-claimed, and by these presents do bargain, sell, remise, and quit-claim unto the said parties of the second part in their actual possession now being, and to their successors in office forever, ALL that certain lot, piece, or parcel of land, situate, lying and being on the farm of the said Cornelius Van Rensselaer, and being the FAMILY BURIAL GROUND OF THE SAID COL. NICHOLAS VAN RENSSELAER so deceased, and is bounded and described as follows, to wit:

BEGINNING at a marble post numbered one (No. 1) which bears south fifty degrees west three feet from the cedar tree standing near the southwest corner of said burial ground, and runs then from said marble post north four degrees west thirty feet to a marble monument or post numbered two (No. 2); thence north eighty-six degrees east eighty-eight feet to a marble monument or post numbered three (No. 3) standing at the west side of the Albany and West Stockbridge Railroad; thence along the same south twenty-one degrees east thirty-one feet and three-quarters of a foot to a marble monument or post numbered four (No. 4), and thence south eighty-six degrees west ninety-seven feet to the place of beginning. Containing two thousand seven hundred and seventy-five feet of ground, together with the right of way and passage to and from said burial ground at all times, through and over the lands of the said Cornelius Van Rensselaer, for the purpose of making interments on said burial ground, or for the purpose of making or repairing the fences enclosing or to enclose said burial ground, or improving, or planting ornamental trees, shrubbery, flowers, or embellishing the ground in any way and manner whatever. With the appurtenances, and all the estate, title and interest therein of the said parties of the first part.

IN WITNESS WHEREOF, the said parties of the first part have hereunto set their hands and seals the day and year first above written.

CORNELIUS VAN RENSSELAER,
MARIA L. VAN RENSSELAER.

Sealed and delivered in the presence of } ELIZABETH B. MANLEY.

STATE OF NEW YORK, RENSSELAER COUNTY, ss.

On this twenty-second day of September, in the year one thousand eight hundred and fifty-seven, before me, the subscriber, appeared Cornelius Van Rensselaer and Maria L., his wife, to me personally known to be the same persons described in, and who executed the within instrument, who severally acknowledged that they executed the same; and the said Maria L., on a private examination by me, apart from her said husband, acknowledged that she executed the same freely, and without any fear or compulsion of her said husband.

    HENRY GOODRICH, Justice of the Peace.

Recorded in the Clerk's Office of the County of Rensselaer the twenty-fifth day of September, 1857, at 12 M., in Book No. 103 of Deeds, on page 239, &c.

        JOHN P. BALL, Clerk.

THIS INDENTURE, made third day of April A. D. one thousand eight hundred and sixty-five, BETWEEN Joachim P. Staats, of the town of Schodack, county of Rensselaer and State of New York, of the first part, and " The Reformed Protestant Dutch Congregation of Greenbush, in the county of Rensselaer," in said State, party of the second part,

WITNESSETH, That the said party of the first part, for and in consideration of the express trusts and behests hereinafter vested in and committed to said party of the second part, hath granted, bargained, sold, remised, released and confirmed, and by these presents doth grant, bargain, sell, remise, release and confirm unto the said party of the second part, their successors and assigns forever, ALL that certain tract, piece or parcel of land, situate, lying and being in said town of Schodack, known and distinguished as THE FAMILY BURIAL GROUND of Joachim P. Staats, the party aforesaid, and described and bounded as follows, that is to say:

BEGINNING at a point at the southwest corner of said lot, two chains, nineteen and one-half links distant from the northwest corner of the dwelling-house of said Joachim P. Staats, in which he now resides, on a course north twenty-two degrees thirty minutes east, and thence runs south seventy-one degrees twenty minutes east, one chain; thence north eighteen degrees forty minutes east, seventy-five links; thence north seventy-one degrees twenty minutes west, one chain; thence south eighteen degrees forty minutes west, seventy-five links to the place of beginning. Containing about one-tenth of an acre of land, be the same more or less, together with all and singular, the tenements, hereditaments and appurtenances thereunto belonging, or in any wise appertaining; and the reversion and reversions, remainder and remainders, rents, issues and profits thereof, and all the estate, right, title, interest, property possession, claim and demand whatsoever, as well at law as in equity, of the said party of the first part, of in or to the above-described premises, and every part and parcel thereof, with the appurtenances, together with a right of way, access and approaching to and from said premises, with teams or otherwise, over and through the lands now belonging to said party of the first part, from the public highway, which said right of way shall be the same route as the one now used by said party of the first part, or as necessarily changed hereafter by him or his heirs; and said party of the second part, their successors or assigns, SHALL AT ALL TIMES have the right to pass or repass thereby on foot, or with horses, wagons, sleighs or other vehicle, or carriage whatever to said land from the public highway.

To have and to hold, all and singular, the above-mentioned and described premises, together with the appurtenances, and the aforesaid easement unto the said party of the second part, their successors and assigns forever, in trust, however, for the benefit of said party of the first part, his heirs and next of kin. The object and intention of this conveyance, and a part of the consideration whereby the said party of the first part makes the same, is, that said land may always and forever be held by said congregation as the sacred depository of the remains of the family, friends and kindred of the party of the first part, and that the said burial ground may never be used for any other purpose whatsoever; and the said party of the first part, for himself, his heirs, executors and administrators, doth covenant, grant and agree to and with the said party of the second part, their successors or assigns, that at the time of making this conveyance, he is the lawful owner of the premises above granted, and that he is seized of a good and indefeasible estate of inheritance therein, and that they are free and clear of inchoate dower rights, and of all incumbrances whatsoever, and the above-granted premises in the quiet and peaceable possession of the said party of the second part, their successors and assigns, against every person whomsoever he and they will and shall warrant and forever defend.

In witness whereof, the said party of the first part has hereunto set his hand and seal the day and year first above written.

JOACHIM P. STAATS.

Sealed and delivered } GROVE P. JENKS.
in presence of

STATE OF NEW YORK, RENSSELAER COUNTY, ss.

On this third day of April, A. D. 1865, before me, the subscriber, a Justice of the Peace of said county, personally appeared Joachim P. Staats, who acknowledged that he executed the foregoing instrument; and I further certify that I know the person who made the said acknowledgment to be the individual described in and who executed the said instrument.

N. N. SEAMAN, Justice of the Peace.

Recorded in Rensselaer County Clerk's office June 24th, 1865, at 12 hours M., in Book of Deeds No. 127, page 463, &c.

EDWIN BRONERDT, Clerk.

PATROON-RENT—RELEASE.

Received, Albany May 6th, 1878, of the Consistory of the Reformed Protestant Church of East Greenbush $7.26 on account of rent on farm leased to Caleb Hill, Nov. 11th, 1793, and $1.24 for interest, and $15.00 as a deposit, the interest of which amount will be an equivalent for the further rents on four acres of said lease. W. S. CHURCH.

Signed and sealed
$ 7.26   In presence of
  1.24   JACOB KIMMEY.
 15.00
―――――
$23.50

RENSSELAER COUNTY, TOWN OF GREENBUSH, ss.

On this sixth day of May, 1878, before me came Jacob Kimmey, to me known, the subscribing witness within-named, who being by me sworn, did depose and say that he resides in the town of Schodack, county aforesaid, that he knows Walter S. Church, the signer of the above receipt therein, and knows him to be the person who is described in and who executed the above instrument, that he was present and saw the said Walter S. Church execute the same, and that he thereupon subscribed his name as a witness thereto.

J. F. GILMAN, Justice of the Peace.

Recorded on the twenty-fifth day of November, 1878, at 10.15 o'clock A. M. in Liber 181 of Deeds, at page 237 and examined.

JAMES KEENAN, Clerk.

CENTENNIAL OF THE REFORMED CHURCH.

EAST GREENBUSH, N. Y., NOV. 17, 1887.

OFFICERS. — *Minister* —— ——. *Elders*—Jacob M. Cotton, Jacob Schermerhorn, Andrew Tweedale, William H. Rhoda. *Deacons*—John Moore, Alexander Traver, Michael H. Warner, Thomas Black. *Sec'y*—Stephen S. Miller. *Treas.*—Jacob Kimmey.

As the one hundred years of history was being rounded out the Church, unfortunately, was without a pastor. Dr. Steele had been laid aside from active duty by a paralytic stroke, had resigned, and moved away.

A few ladies were particularly zealous to observe the Centennial, and they soon kindled the enthusiasm of some of the gentlemen, and the exercises were decided upon.

The following gentlemen were chosen a committee in charge: Jacob M. Cotton, John Moore and Jesse P. Van Ness.

They issued the appended circular letter and sent it to many old members and friends of the Church:

A. D. 1787.   CENTENNIAL.   A. D. 1887.

Reformed Church of East Greenbush, N. Y.

Wednesday and Thursday, Nov. 16th and 17th.

Rev. Edward A. Collier, D.D., Presiding.

Nov. 16th. 2 P. M.—Sermon in the Holland language.
Voorleser and Singers

Nov. 17th. 10.30 A. M.—Centennial Sermon by a grandson of the first pastor.

2 P. M.—Historical Address. Also addresses or letters by ex-Pastors or their representatives.

7 P. M.—Addresses by members of Classis, visiting clergymen and others. Also a Poem written for the occasion.

You are cordially invited to attend.

J. P. VAN NESS, Corresponding Secretary.

Many accepted this invitation and large audiences attended the services, when the following order of exercises was carried out:

ORDER OF EXERCISES.

Wednesday Afternoon, Nov. 16th.
2 o'clock.

Rev. Edward A. Collier, D. D., Presiding.

Holland Services as our fathers worshipped one hundred years ago.
Singing—Psalm 98: 2—In Holland Language.
Reading of Ten Commandments and Scripture Selection.
By Voorleser Mr. J. Backer.
Singing—Psalm 25: 6.
Prayer—In English Language.
Singing—Ps. 116: 7, 8.—Collection taken during Singing.
Sermon—In Holland language, by Rev. Lawrence Dykstra, of the Holland Church, Albany, N. Y.
Prayer—By Elder A. M. Donner.
Singing—Hymn, in English.
Benediction.

Thursday Morning, Nov. 17th.
10.30 o'clock.

Anthem—"Praise the Lord, O Jerusalem"—By the Choir.
Invocation.
Scripture Reading.
Singing—Hymn 362.
Prayer.
Singing—"In the secret of His presence," - - - - Stebbins.
By Mrs. W. J. Bentley.
Sermon—By Rev. J. Romeyn Berry, D. D., of Rhinebeck, N. Y.
Singing—"When the mists have cleared away," - - Henshaw.
By Mrs. W. J. Bentley.
Addresses or letters by ex-Pastors.
Prayer.
Anthem—"Crown Him Lord of all"—By the Choir.
Benediction.

Thursday Afternoon, 2 o'clock.

Organ Voluntary.
Anthem—By the Choir—"O, how lovely."
Invocation.
Scripture Reading.
Response—"The Book is open."
Prayer.
Singing—"Jesus lover of my soul"—By Mrs. W. J Bentley.
Historical Address—By Rev. J. F. Yates, A. M., of Fort Edward, N. Y.
Singing—Hymn 104.
Addresses by Members of Classis.
Prayer.
Singing—"One sweetly solemn thought" - - - - Ambrose.
Mrs. Bentley.
Benediction.

CENTENNIAL EXERCISES. 33

Thursday Evening, 7 o'clock.

Organ Voluntary.
Solo—"Oh! for the wings of a dove"—By Mrs. Willard Sproug.
Invocation.
Scripture Reading.
Singing—Hymn by Mrs. Anna Romeyn Taylor.
Prayer.
Anthem—"The Church rejoices"—By the Choir.
Addresses—10 minutes :
Rev. E. Lodewick—"The Reformed Church in relation to other Churches."
Rev. P. T. Pockman—"The Reformed Church and Education."
Rev. W. F. Anderson—"The Reformed Church and Missions."
Fraternal Greetings—By visiting Clergymen.
Singing—Hymn 931.
Original Poem—Written by Rev. Norman Plass—Read by Rev. Edward A. Collier, D. D.
Closing Prayer.
Doxology.

Praise the name of God most high,
Praise Him, all below the sky;
Praise Him, all ye heavenly host,
Father, Son, and Holy Ghost;
As through countless ages past,
Evermore His name shall last.

Benediction.

HYMN.

[Written by Mrs. Anna Romeyn Taylor, daughter of the firs minister of Reformed Church, Greenbush.]

On God's own mount a temple stands,
A house all glorious in His eyes,
Eternal, and unmade with hands,
Which His own presence sanctifies.

[3]

There sing the seraphs—there are bowed
   The white-robed elders, and the throng
Of humble worshipers, who crowd
   Those temple gates, to join their song.

There sits the Lamb—He lights the place,
   His glory radiates the scene;
And in the trophies of His grace
   His Father's promised gift is seen.

And will He—can He condescend
   To leave those heights and dwell with man?
Prostrate in dust our spirits bend,
   And wonder at the Gospel plan.

Yet we will plead His promised grace,
   And though no worthiness we claim,
Upon these walls and in this place
   We'll ask Him to re-write His name.

Come, dearest Lord, and in this hour
   The influence of Thy grace impart;
Come in Thy Spirit's mighty power,
   And animate with zeal each heart.

CENTENNIAL SERMON.

By Rev. J. Romeyn Berry, D.D.

But unto the Son He saith, Thy throne, O God, is forever and ever—Hebrews 1:8.

OUR anniversaries are reminders of our frailty. Each one is a memorial of a vanished past. The symbols which they suggest are the morning flower, the withered grass, the shuttle, the vapor, the dream, the watch in the night.

When the review covers, as in the present instance, the field of a century, the impression of transitoriness is only more intense. The prophet's question rises spontaneously to our lips, "The fathers, where are they?" The sky and hills and streams remain, but where are the men and women and children who a hundred years ago trod these hills and looked upward to this sky, or sailed on yonder stream? It is the average lifetime of three generations. It embraces many a change in the pulpit, the pew, and at the Communion Table. If you call the roll of most of the worshipers of this church, innumerable grave-stones rise up to respond for the names of the sleepers at their feet. The living are only a few survivors of a great departed past. We gather as the remnants of regiments have gathered recently at Gettysburg, to erect monuments for battles long since fought, and for comrades long ago turned to dust.

All this is naturally humiliating and saddening. It tells of frailty and mortality and change and loss. But is there nothing but themes like these before us at such an hour? Have we no topic of courage or joy or hope? Yes, "in all these things we are more than conquerors through Him that loved us." We come to this centennial to speak not of defeat but triumph; not of death but life; not of mortal man but the everlasting God. The centuries are God's; the Church is God's; the saints past or present are God's; we are God's. All the incomprehensible wonders of His existence and power are gathered around our feebleness like a wall of fire round about us and a glory in the midst of us. We glory only in Him—not in our godly ancestors, for whom we bless Him, and who may be a silent crowd of witnesses around this scene to-day. But not in them do we glory—we glory only in the Lord. As the apostle gloried in his infirmity that the power of Christ might rest on him, so do we who are so compassed with infirmity and who die daily, glory only in the unchangeable perfect-ness of Jehovah and in the unfading splendors of His majesty.

> "Great God, our lowliness takes heart to play
> Beneath the shadows of thy state;
> The only comfort of our littleness
> Is that Thou art so great."

A special aspect and application of this thought comes before us to-day. It is the memorial day of a church of Jesus Christ. The most of its pastors and members have died. The walls of its old sanctuary have long since been scattered to the winds, as these of the present edifice must some day disappear. But the church itself as a part of Christ's kingdom is immortal. Whatever becomes of its material constituents and conditions—though its members should all die, though its local organization should be dissolved, yet so far as this church ever possessed the spiritual elements of Christ's kingdom and thus was a part of that kingdom, it is imperishable. For the life of the church depends not on man but on Christ. The King secures the Kingdom. To the Son Jehovah says, "Thy throne, O God, is forever and ever."

Let us then enter on these centennial services with some thoughts on the relation of Christ's eternal throne to His church upon the earth.

1. Christ is a great King. The ordinary symbol indeed of His relations to our world is the Cross on

which He died. On spire and sepulcher, on necklace and volume, its form is ever before us. And precious are the truths which the Cross represents. The story of God's love and man's salvation is inseparable from that Cross. He who rightly knows its meaning is a theologian; he who rightly feels its power is a saint. No church is a church indeed that cannot with the apostle's heart and meaning use his words, "God forbid that I should glory save in the Cross of our Lord Jesus Christ." But that Cross could never have saved a single soul without that throne, just as the throne could have availed nothing without the Cross. They are eternal allies in the great Kingdom of grace and glory.

2. The throne of the Son is supreme and universal. All power is His in heaven and in earth. All the departments of nature as well as grace are beneath His sway. He upholds all things by the word of His power. Neither angel nor insect flies —neither flood nor dewdrop falls but by His will.

Men speak of God's providence and it is true, but the God of that providence is the Son. The Father has committed all things to the Son, and "given Him a name which is above every name, that at the name of Jesus every knee should bow of things in heaven and things in earth and things under the earth, and that every tongue should confess that Jesus Christ is Lord, to the glory of God the Father."

This is a great truth, not only for the church, but for the whole race to ponder, that the entire system of nature to-day is beneath the supreme control of the God-Man, Christ Jesus. This is the central fact without which all this world's history is a riddle which no philosophy can solve.

We know how hopelessly men were perplexed in astronomy until Copernicus taught them that the sun and not the earth was the center of the solar system, and afterward Newton and Kepler added their illustrious lessons to the science. Then everything came right—every movement of planet or satellite, every eclipse, every change was part of a great harmony governed by infallible laws perfectly explained.

So in the complicated and mysterious movements of this world's history. As long as we try to make man the center and master of the scene, or nature her own law-giver, or chance or fate the arbiters of destiny, everything appears—

> "A dark
> Illimitable ocean, without bound,
> Without dimension, where length, breadth and height,
> And time and place are lost; where Eldest Night
> And Chaos, ancestors of nature, hold
> Eternal anarchy, amidst the noise
> Of endless wars and by confusion stand."

But the moment Christ's throne appears, it is like the ancient fiat, "Let there be light, and there was light." Omnipotence and wisdom and justice and goodness are on that throne. Great purposes of righteousness and grace are there; eternal years are there. Then like the Psalmist we sing, "The Lord reigneth, let the earth rejoice, let the multitude of isles be glad thereof."

It is a delightful truth, that all the dispensations of this world, all its events of joy or sorrow, are beneath the sway of the God-Man, our brother, Jesus Christ. It reminds us of that charming truth in natural science which reveals to us those manifold obligations of our lives to the agency of the natural sun; that not only does he keep the planets in their orbits; not only does he daily warm and illumine and beautify the world; not only does the life of every man and beast and plant depend on his genial rays; not only does he pencil every hue of earth and sky, but through unnumbered ages of the past he has been storing up his own heat and light in all the fuel of our globe, so that not a gas-jet burns, not a furnace glows, not an engine moves, not a train rushes across the land, not a steamer ploughs the ocean, but all comes from the light and heat which the sun long ago stored up for us in those primeval forests which have made the coal-beds of the world.

And has the great Sun of righteousness now on the throne treasured up nothing for us in the past? Was it not in the far past eternity that His love looked down on our ruin? Was it not then that He espoused our cause and covenanted with the Father to be our Redeemer? Was it not well-nigh two thousand years ago that He tabernacled in our nature, bore our griefs, died for our sins, and rose for our justification? Is it not of His fulness that all we have received, and grace for grace? And is He not on that glorious throne just now for the very object of carrying out the eternal purposes of His grace and dispensing the daily and hourly blessings of His love?

Yes, Christ reigns over nature, animate and inanimate, over men and devils, over friend and foe, over joy and sorrow, reigns over every event that befalls us, reigns in righteousness to all, reigns in everlasting love to His saints. "Blessing, and honor, and glory, and power, be unto Him that sitteth upon the throne, and unto the Lamb forever and ever."

3. A conspicuous characteristic of this throne is its peculiar relations to the church.

Its great design is the welfare, triumph and everlasting glory of the church. It is as Head over all things to the church, that Christ fills it. Everything else is subordinate to this. Christ's own reward and glory for the suffering of death, are involved in the Christ's final victory and splendor. Therefore "in Zion is His throne."

When God led Israel through the wilderness He was King of all the earth, yet not in that peculiar way in which He was King of Israel. That tabernacle and mercy-seat, that pillar of cloud and fire, that Urim and Thummim and covenant were not for Egypt or Moab or Philistia, but for Israel alone. Even the prophet of the enemy looking upon the chosen people from the top of Pisgah exclaimed, "Jehovah his God is with him, and the shout of a King is among them."

If the other would share in these special privileges, they must come into Israel's camp and worship Israel's God, for only there was the throne and the glory. So to-day, while Christ is King of Kings, His throne is pre-eminently in His Church and for His Church. To the final glory of that Church He guides all the movements of time with an unerring eye and unwearied hand.

> "And all the kingdoms of the earth
> Shall worship or shall die."

4. The bond which binds Christ's Church to His throne is one of spiritual life and love. "I founded an empire on force," said Napoleon, looking back on the wreck of all his greatness. So stand most of the kingdoms of this world; their pillars are

their soldiery, their arm is an arm of flesh, and in the struggle the strongest takes the throne.

Not so in the Kingdom of Christ in its relation to His saints. The Eternal King communicates His own life to every loyal subject, makes it partaker of His own spirit, kindles within it the flame of a pure and immortal love, and thus unifies the Kingdom in one body, of which the Sovereign is the Head, and the Church the members. There are thousands of parts in that Church, with thousands of nerves and arteries and veins, but one life-blood, one heart-beat, one warmth, one sympathy, one interest in all. The life reaches not only through every land and age of earth, but goes on into heaven and eternity. It binds all the saints, past, present and to come, in one great phalanx of life and love. It kindles in all hearts the purest and highest enthusiasm of gratitude and loyalty to the Lamb in the midst of the throne. The universal cry is, "Thou art worthy, for thou wast slain, and hast redeemed us to God by thy blood out of every kindred, and tongue, and people, and nation."

The world has seen many a noted instance of soldiers' devotion to military leaders, as when one of Napoleon's heroes said to the surgeon who was probing near his heart for a musket-ball, "Go a little deeper and you will find the emperor there." A few weeks ago in Berlin, at the anniversary of the death of Marshal Blucher (who saved Wellington at Waterloo), an aged soldier who had fought under the Marshal laid a wreath of oak leaves at the feet of the statue of his old commander.

It is well that earthly love and gratitude from man to man should be expressed. But all this is nothing to the purer emotions of the true believer for the Lord who bought him. The smoke of stake and scaffold; the horrors of the amphitheater; the agonies of the rack; the tortures of the Cross have told the world the story of christian love for Jesus, the King and Captain of Salvation.

> "They met the tyrant's brandished steel,
> The lion's gory mane,
> They bowed their necks the death to feel;
> Who follows in their train?"

The whole church of the truly regenerate and sanctified—millions upon millions of faithful hearts who have been willing, if need be, to lay down their lives for their Redeemer. If we are not heroes and martyrs every day, as some days have seen them, it is not that the spirit of heroism and martyrdom does not exist. There are as many true hearts in the army to-day as ever, and more. The same spirit, developed sometimes in one form of fidelity and sometimes another, according to circumstances, pervades all the ranks of the sacramental host. Let the occasions come, and England's Smithfields and Spain's Inquisitions and Rome's wild beasts would find as splendid consecrations to Jesus as the world ever saw,—that the spirit of that King who once himself hung on the Cross, is in the breast of all His followers.

So the armies of the Lamb move on from generation to generation, from century to century; so church after church celebrates the memorials of its history and sings the triumphs of its King.

That was a sublime scene in our National Capital at the close of the late war, when the different loyal armies met and held their grand review. For two days the tramp of that mighty host was heard from morning to night. The broad avenue was filled from morning to night with their outspread ranks, from side to side, and as far down as the eye could reach, on and on they came, company after company, regiment after regiment, corps, army; soldiers from East, West, North, and from the South too. Many of them born in foreign lands, many were the languages of the mighty host. Thousands of miles apart had their battles been; tens of thousands of their comrades had fallen in the strife. But from year to year the ranks had been replenished with new recruits. In one great cause had they fought; in one great victory they had shared; one Union had they saved. In its glad Capital they were met, and on and on they came; one incessant shout of a Nation's thanks fell every moment on their ears. Before the eyes of the nation's ruler every soldier marched. To the enjoyment of the rewards of their victory, in homes of love and a land of peace, they all passed on.

It was a picture of higher things. A grander march is ever going on; an army not composed of one nation alone, but of all nations and kindreds and peoples and tongues; not in one land alone, but in all lands; not for two days only, but for day and night through endless years. At this very moment the sun on our side of the globe and the stars on the other are looking down on these hosts. Every language, every shade of color, every condition of social life are represented in those ranks. But in the same great cause are they enlisted, one great Commander is over all. In one great triumph shall they share. Before one great throne shall they pass in final review, and in one great land of peace and glory shall they reap their everlasting reward.

In this great march of Christ's army, this church has joined one hundred years. Its battle-flag at the beginning and now is that which its King gave it, with the charge, "Be thou faithful unto death and I will give thee the crown of life." Many of its officers and members have kept that charge and won that crown. Not one of its original veterans remains. The last of these long ago passed into the joy of the Lord. Over and over again have its ranks had to be renewed. But there is no change in the cause, commission or nature of the conflict; the Great Commander is the same and His throne is forever and ever.

Standing then at the end of this church's century and amid such relations to the throne of the Messiah, what is the lesson which should impress itself on every heart? Surely it is *Loyalty*.

In the recent centennial celebration of our National Independence, and later of our National Constitution—in every monument erected on battle-fields and every statue of the heroes of those battles, one great design has been to stimulate the spirit of patriotism, of love and loyalty to our country. And surely in a day like this, we can adopt no lower formula of duty towards the throne of our Lord and Saviour. Loyalty thus renewed, loyalty to Jesus Christ is the lesson of this hour.

But how shall this loyalty be described? First, it is loyalty to His Truth. This is the Church's first duty. The Word that comes from that throne is her supreme and only rule. Her law is what Christ commands—her faith what Christ reveals. Her unchangeable commission is to keep His words and preach His Gospel, not fancies of presumptuous ministers, nor the unsanctified conceits of foolish members, but the glorious Gospel of the ever-blessed God. The army's marching orders are not from the ranks, but from the Commander. The dreams of men vanish with the night that creates them. The Great King says, "Heaven and earth shall pass away, but my words shall not pass away." What malignant assaults has infidelity made upon this Word during this past century, and what changes in the weapons and mode of assault! Yet what harm has all this bitter warfare done to this Word of Christ? What statement has it disproved? What doctrine impaired? There it stands firm as the rock of ages, and true as ever in the language of the King, "Whosoever shall fall upon this stone shall be broken, but on whomsoever it shall fall it shall grind him to powder." Science has made and is constantly making many noble discoveries, but none as yet have shaken this great rock. The hypotheses unfriendly to Revelation which some illustrious names have announced and along the line of which they thought they saw a refutation of some of the teachings of the Bible, have not on further investigation worked out the results which they expected. So that a learned scientific professor recently said, "Much of the work of Huxley has already become obsolete; some of it condemned by himself; and there are few prominent scientists who have not frequently found the searcher unpleasantly detecting their errors."*

And all this rise and fall of boasted theories within a dozen years! But during the nearly two thousand years since Jesus spoke, what word of His has become obsolete? What error of His has "the searcher" found?

It is to this high and immortal truth of its Eternal Lord that the Church of Christ and the ministry of Christ are dedicated—"separated unto the Gospel of God," as Paul describes himself. It was in fidelity to this Gospel and against the traditions and commandments of men that the Mother Church in Holland gave her sixty thousand martyrs to her Lord, fought the armies of Romanism in a war of eighty years, cut the dykes and let the ocean roll over her fields and towns rather than the tide of a false faith; and her worshipers even gathered in an upper room to hear the preaching of the Word of Christ, when the only light they had for their service was that which came from the fires outside, which were burning one of their number at the stake for fidelity to this same Word.

Oh, with such an ancestry and with such examples before them, there is no church in the world which ought to be more loyal to the Word of the Lord than this Daughter of Holland—the Reformed

---

* Professor Macloskie, Presbyterian Review, October, 1887.

[4]

Church in America. Amid the evanescence of all earthly things, here is the incorruptible Word which liveth and abideth forever. "For all flesh is as grass, and all the glory of man as the flower of grass. The grass withereth and the flower thereof falleth away: but the Word of the Lord endureth forever. And this is the Word which by the Gospel is preached unto you." It has already, as we have said, the dominion of universal power, but it seeks the dearer dominion of universal love.

Another vital element of loyalty to the throne of Christ has aspect to the aggressive spirit of that throne. It is a throne of conquest not over bodies merely, but hearts. Its aim is universal victory. Manifold and malignant are its foes, but "as I live, saith the Lord, every knee shall bow to Me." This world has been redeemed; it shall be reclaimed. The trophies of the Cross shall all be brought before the throne. The provisions are sure. Sin and Satan shall be vanquished. Righteousness shall reign; salvation shall triumph; the whole world shall acknowledge the Lord whom once it crucified. We know not when nor exactly how, but we do know the fact that—

> "The King who reigns in Zion's towers
> Shall all the world command."

To accomplish this end, His Church is to pray and labor night and day. As He ascended that throne,

He gave as His last great commission, "Go ye into all the world and preach the Gospel to every creature." To every disciple He says "Go." To the sinful and sad, He says "Come." But when one has come and received His mercy, then He says "Go." To the leper, the blind, the demoniac, the guilty, the lost—"Go tell what the Lord hath done for thee; go tell other lost ones of the love and the salvation; go be a witness and a messenger of my mercy to a perishing world."

To this high end every disciple is called in some way to diffuse the knowledge of his King and Saviour. For this purpose the Church exists; not merely to enjoy its own comfortable sanctuaries and sweet Sabbaths and precious hopes and happy centennials, but to be ever active and aggressive in winning the world to Christ—as light to shine, as a witness to testify, as an army to advance and conquer.

Every church and every believer in christendom to-day owe their spiritual life and hope to the aggressive and faithful labors of some who had gone before. How came this church in existence? How came you and I to be Christians? We are all the fruits of missionary, and foreign missionary labors. We are all the results of somebody's obedience to the King's command, "Go." For what was our ancestry? Not very long ago they were brutal savages, "having no hope and without God in the world." Imagine your ancestors standing closely in a row in front of this pulpit down yonder aisle. How far would that line extend before it would contain a half-clothed savage worshiping an image of wood or stone? Not as far as yonder threshold, and that savage would be one of your forefathers! But a faithful missionary brought to him the message of Christ's love, and so the Gospel from generation to generation came on, until to-day you are a child of God, and so this church arose and has lived a hundred years!

What is the lesson which gratitude suggests but that of a larger and gladder consecration than ever before to that great work by which and for which the church exists. Proclaim the glories of your King throughout the world. Lay your prayers and offerings at His feet. Lay your hearts and lives there. Bring your trophies of salvation there. Let not only this surrounding community know how you love and serve your King—let distant lands know it; let India, China and Japan know it; let Heaven know it; let it be such that you yourself shall know it when you shall come to appear before the throne of your King, that He may give you everlasting rewards for your devoted loyalty to Him.

Dear friends, this is a day of gladness, of gratitude and of lofty impulse. A century of God's goodness and grace to this church has passed. What shall the next century reveal? what growth? what power? what fidelity to Christ? Shall it live with a new fervor, give with a new liberality, and labor with a new zeal? Shall it be so consecrated to Christ and such a co-worker with Him in His Kingdom, that "when His glory shall be revealed, ye may be glad also with exceeding joy?" For be assured that glory shall be revealed. These centuries are rapidly bringing in the crowning day of earth's great King. There is no doubt about His splendid and universal triumph. Earthly kings may be dethroned or die; earthly kingdoms may be wrecked. The world is full of shattered thrones and crowns in the dust. One of the saddest but most beautiful pieces of modern sculpture is that statue of Napoleon which represents the sick exile in his arm chair with the map of Europe on his knees. The keen eye and stern brow and compressed lip are still there, but health has gone, power, glory. That map was once his chess-board, where he moved kings and queens and knights and crowns as he chose. But soon not an inch of its soil and not a soldier could he call his own. And since that hour what new dethronements and changes have there been on that same map!

But amid all the upheavals of human thrones the

throne of Jesus widens its sway and expands its glory every year. Never were its predicted splendors so near their manifestations as at this very moment of our celebration. As we speak the glory draws nigh. Perhaps long before this church shall celebrate its second century the King himself shall come, and heaven and earth shall join in the shout, "The kingdoms of this world are become the kingdoms of our Lord and of His Christ, and He shall reign forever and ever!"

Dr. Berry was the grandson of the first pastor. He died suddenly at Asbury Park, N. J., on Friday, June 5, 1891. On Wednesday evening, June 3d, he had preached the synodical sermon as the retiring President of General Synod, and on Thursday evening, June 4, he had joined in the Communion service. Suddenly he was bidden to go up higher and take his seat at the marriage supper of the Lamb.

After the sermon, the Rev. P. Q. Wilson, the only one of the two living pastors present, delivered the following address.

REV. P. Q. WILSON'S ADDRESS.

The centennial came in with a sharp breeze. The mountain tops were covered with snow. But although a little late in the season, we are glad that it has arrived. Smiles and good cheer beam forth from every countenance. And the people! Multitudes upon multitudes! Just like East Greenbush. Everyone seems to be impelled by a grand motive. Even the bell-ringer gave the old bell an extra swing.

> "Ring, sing, ring, sing, pleasant Sabbath bell,
> Chime, rhyme, chime, rhyme, over dale and dell;
> Rhyme, ring, chime, sing, pleasant Sabbath bell,
> Chime, sing, rhyme, ring, over field and fell."

And upon this bright autumnal morning many pleasant thoughts come trooping up upon the field of memory. Our hearts are full of the great and good things of the past and present. From the vista of by-gone years we evoke the moral grandeur of consecrated lives—it shall speak to the living.

When I entered upon my ministry here in 1861, I noticed that this congregation exhibited a great deal of good common sense. Their economy was seen in the design and the execution of this substantial edifice—a church built for time. From foundation to dome the whole structure, in its material and style, may well remind us of the solid Dutch people, and the old-fashioned Calvinistic theology. There was a look of thrift and intelligence, that commanded the attention of thoughtful minds, upon surrounding things. The salary was sensible; there was money in the treasury; we sold the pews and paid the debt. There were twelve pastors in the century and each minister contributed some good things towards making this church in her pride and beauty. I was the first pastor in the new church—beautiful for situation. East Greenbush affords a commanding view of the surrounding country.

On the north, there nestled beneath the hills, the famous city of Troy and the proud capital of your own State. On the west the wide sweeping valley of the Hudson charms the eye. Beyond the river the Helderberg and the Catskill mountain ranges present a bold prospect; and here, all around, are the homes of plenty and farmers living in comfort and opulence. And your church, so complete in all its apartments, has been reared and adorned by the sturdy farmers, the sons and daughters of the soil. And as I survey your recent work of repairs, I readily conclude that this is the fullest, the brightest and the handsomest centennial that I have ever attended. There is the iron fence; the children sang and we gathered together the money. It stands firm and strong. Always remember the children; don't forget the poor. They will be your coadjutors by and by. The attendance upon our Sabbath services was praiseworthy, almost every pew occupied upon the Lord's day. And it is expected that the rising generation, stimulated by the noble record of former years, will vigorously maintain, in its pristine beauty, the name and character of this Reformed Church.

I also witnessed your hospitality. This church has always been noted for its care of the pastor. The tables were loaded; the hearts overflowed in kindness and good will. I do not wonder that so many clergyman are looking towards East Greenbush. No one prays here, "Keep our minister humble and we will keep him poor." The donations were the outbursts of generosity—long may they live. Our social gatherings, our wedding feasts, and our presents will be remembered. Our young people in all their relations gave great promise for the future. "The hand that rocks the cradle rules the world."

This church not only gave gifts, but she has given more. Three of her sons within a few years have been equipped for the ministry. They are here to-day. And the Methodist Church and parsonage are a credit to the property and religious character of the village.

I am at home to-day! Familiar faces, familiar things. And this celebration will note an important era in the history of each of our lives. An epoch in the history of your church to which you and your children will turn with fond remembrance; and at every advance of your progressive religious life, you are forcibly reminded of two things closely knit together—faith and works. Liberal hands spread the table to-day. The young women, sharing the disposition of their good mothers, have given largely from basket and store. 'Tis work, work, work, and hence we have here a succession of devoted people following on in the line of religious duties. This is the hope of your church. The centuries are thus welded together by an unbroken chain of men and women actuated and regulated by the scriptural ideas of truth and duty. You stand to-day upon an eminence of privilege and prospect.

But while we all rejoice, the feelings of sadness rise unbidden in our hearts because so many of our friends and neighbors have departed to return no more. The cemetery is filling up.

> "I like that good old Saxon phrase,
>   Which calls the burial ground God's acre. 'Tis just.
> It consecrates each grave within its walls,
>   And breathes a benison o'er its sleeping dust."

The fathers, where are they? The mothers, where are they? The exuberance of our joy is restrained by the collection of the vast harvest which death has gathered here.

> "When we remember well
>   The friends so linked together,
> That we have seen around us fall,
>   Like leaves in wintry weather."

But their memory is precious, while the mantle of their faith and industry has fallen upon their descendants, who will carry the ark of this Zion into the future conflicts of truth and righteousness. And all this is the outgrowth of good preaching. And as we conclude, we look all around. The work is well done; the Consistory deserve praise; the committee, our thanks; the choir, our respects; the carpenter has done his work well and the sexton is obliging. All stand upon their merit from pulpit to pew. Even the ministers carry in their faces a dignity and reverence becoming this memorable occasion. You can only celebrate one centennial; and will you, as the custodians of this house of the Lord, prepare to hand down the great work of this vast congregation to your successors, unimpaired by the rapid flight of time, remembering that the ultimate end and object of all church work is the conversion of sinful man to Christ, not the wearing of gold or apparel, but the ornaments of a meek and quiet spirit. There were twelve pastors in the century, and the Lord has permitted your humble servant, the only one of the twelve, to come and participate in these festivities, and say to the past, rich in ancient and historic lore, in faith and prayer, in word and deed, "vale amice, vale amice," and congratulate you all as a people and a church as you step over into the second century of your church life.

A letter was read from Rev. John Steele, D.D., the last pastor, which in his feeble state of health, he had dictated. It ran in these touching lines.

DR. STEELE'S LETTER.

NEWARK, N. J., Nov. 7, 1887.

My Dear Christian Brethren and Friends of the Reformed Church and Congregation at East Greenbush, N. Y.:

I had fondly hoped, and, until a comparatively recent date, rather confidently expected to be present at the centennial celebration of your church, but as the days and months of the advancing year have rolled by, it has become more and more apparent that my state of health would not allow the fatigue of the journey, or the natural excitement of the occasion.

But although not permitted, in the Providence of God, to be present with you in person and take part in the interesting exercises and glad festivities of the time, yet I cannot resist the inclination to send you, at least, my cordial greetings and warm congratulations, that God, in his Providence, has brought you to so interesting a period in the history of your beloved church, permitting you to commemorate, in this fitting manner, the centennial year of the church's existence. For more than two years I have looked forward with deep interest to this celebration. In view of my official relation to the church, I had expected to spend time, thought, and a labor of love in the preparation of a memorial discourse.

Although the materials for such a discourse were quite meagre, yet I hoped, with what I had, and with what I might still be able to gather, to produce something which would, at least, be appropriate to the occasion, and perhaps prove of some value as giving to the church at large a small contribution to the history of one of the venerable churches of our denomination.

Those of you, Christian friends, who were present at our joyous harvest home festival, a little more than a year ago, will remember that I made a distinct reference to the approaching centennial of the church, which you are now privileged to celebrate, and which, in the excellent health that I then enjoyed, I so confidently expected to carry forward to the best of my ability and make it, if possible, a grand success. Few things, indeed, in the course of my ministry have been more delightful in the contemplation, than the prospect of closing up the century with you, and, if the Lord willed, to minister to you for a time, at least, at the beginning of the second century of your existence. But, at a most unexpected moment, I was stricken down. The hand of God touched me, and all active service in the ministry was suddenly brought to a close. I shall not say more at this point, as you know the rest. Whether the Master will have any more work for me to do in His vineyard, in seeking to alarm the careless, comfort christians, and guide inquiring sinners to the Saviour, He only knows, and will make it manifest in His own time. Until then, we will try by His grace to wait with patience and unmurmuring submission. The way sometimes seems dark, but "we follow where our Father leads, and trust where we cannot see." His Providence and ways are wise. Infinite wisdom and goodness must ever characterize all the allotments of the Divine hand.

> "Behind a frowning providence
> He hides a smiling face."

But I must not write a lengthy communication. I have already exceeded the limits I had laid out for myself. Had I been permitted, as on former occasions, in leaving the churches I have served, to take formal leave of this congregation, I could have said many things which I cannot write. But the pastoral relation between myself and this church has been dissolved in God's own time and way, and He will, I am sure, send you a man after His own heart, to break unto you the bread of life. You are no longer my people, as I was happy to call you; I am no longer your pastor. But allow me to say that, as a family, we have, and shall continue to have, while life shall last, very precious memories of this church and congregation. Ten of the best years of my life were spent among you. For your uniform attention and love, and for your unnumbered acts of thoughtful kindness and tender ministrations, I thank God, and I thank you. Never can we possibly forget the unwearying assiduity, with which you strove to relieve my distress, during those long and weary months which immediately followed the afflictive dispensation by which I was brought low. These countless acts of affectionate regard at your hands, are engraven upon the tablets of memory, never to be effaced. Truer and more constant friends we have never had, nor shall ever find in this world. But we have parted—

> "Time can never
> Bring the faded past again.
> Like the wave of some lone river,
> It is buried in the main.
> We have parted, yet we linger
> Where the light of memory plays,
> As that wizard, solemn finger
> Wanders back to other days.
> Then farewell, yet oh,
> Watch o'er us, Father,
> On the land or sea ;
> Till the weary way before us
> Bears us up, at last, to Thee.

And now, brethren, I commend you to God, and to the word of His grace, which is able to build you up, and to give you an inheritance among all them which are sanctified. May the God of peace, that brought again from the dead our Lord Jesus, that great Shepherd of the sheep, through the blood of the everlasting covenant, make you perfect in every good work to do His will, working in you that which is well pleasing in His sight, through Jesus Christ.

Affectionately,
JOHN STEELE.

Dr. Steele died at his home in Newark, N. J., January 17, 1889.

LETTER FROM REV. F. N. ZABRISKIE, D.D.

PRINCETON, N. J., Nov. 15, 1887.

Mr. J. P. Van Ness, Sec'y.

DEAR SIR:—I thank you for your courteous invitation to be present at the centennial celebration of the Reformed Church of East Greenbush on the 16th and 17th of this month. I regret that I am unable to attend an occasion of so much interest to myself, as well as to those who are more immediately concerned. I have never been at your church or village, but they are both of them sacred places in my associations and my affection. There my venerated grandfather, James V. C. Romeyn, began his ministry; and there my mother, his eldest child, was born. There also one whom I loved and honored as an uncle, the Rev. Dr. Benj. C. Taylor, began his long and useful work as a pastor.

Of the latter two, I do not suppose that I can add anything but my personal tribute of reverence and affection to what will be told by the historian, the preacher, and others who shall be present at the centennial observance. I knew my grandfather only in his last years of extreme infirmity, both of body and mind, and I was then a very little boy. But I have the vision before my memory of a beautiful old man, with a face as pure and beaming as a child's, and yet moving about in his decrepitude with the dignity of a patriarch.

Of my mother, it would not become me to speak at length, or to utter the feelings of my heart. I wish merely to say that in force of character, in strength and quickness of mind, in vivacity and sensibleness of conversation, and above all, in nobility, generosity and humble piety of spirit, she was one whom Greenbush may well be proud to claim as a daughter, even as I am proud to call her my mother.

May God grant to old Greenbush Church many such pastors as Romeyn and Taylor in the coming century; many such ministers' wives as Susan Van Vranken Romeyn and Anna Romeyn Taylor; and many such ministers' daughters as Susan Van

Campen Romeyn, the wife of George Zabriskie, and the mother of . Yours faithfully,

FRANCIS NICOLL ZABRISKIE.

Rev. F. N. Zabriskie, D.D., died at Princeton, N. J., May 13, 1891, in the 60th year of his age.

LETTER READ FROM DR. GRIFFIS.

BOSTON, Sept. 19, '87.

Mr. Jesse P. Van Ness, Cor. Sec'y, Centennial Committee, East Greenbush Reformed Church.:

DEAR SIR:—Reading in the *Christian Intelligencer* of the centennial celebration of the East Greenbush Reformed Church, to be held November 17, the memory of very pleasant days spent among your people during the years 1866 and '67 came vividly to my mind, and I cannot forbear sending you greetings and good wishes.

While a student in Rutgers College, I visited the home of my classmate, now the Rev. Edward Lodewick, and enjoyed the hospitalities of several of the good people of the congregation, and of the pastor, Rev. William Anderson, and his family. I remember speaking in the Sabbath School several times, and I think also on my return from Japan, eight years later, I lectured in the church, and again met some of the people.

It is because I have such a happy remembrance of the church and people that I am tempted to add my testimony to the warm-heartedness of the East Greenbush people, and to say that I have a love for the Reformed Church which prompts me to join with you in spirit on your centennial anniversary day, and pray for a continuance of the Divine favor upon you all as you enter upon your second century of history.

In sincere sympathy with your honored pastor in his affliction, I remain, with a warm love for the Reformed Church, and in the patience and kingdom of Jesus Christ,

WM. ELLIOT GRIFFIS,

Pastor of the Shawmut Congregational Church, Boston, formerly domine of the Reformed Church, Schenectady, N. Y.

JEREMIAH F. YATES.

HISTORICAL ADDRESS.

By Rev. Jeremiah F. Yates.

THE Banian, the sacred fig tree of India, is a thing of centuries. It is a spectacle of wonder and beauty, a pillared temple of the plain, carpeted with verdure, ceiled with foliage and frescoed with flowers and fruit. The beasts of the field seek its grateful shade, fowls of varied wing find refuge in its mazy depths and feed upon its perennial supplies. Every bough is at once a result and a factor. Not content to be only a bough; it bends to the ground as if in prayer, and the answering earth draws down its fibers into roots and starts a new trunk into the air world. And the process has no end. All other trees bear in themselves the sentence of their decay and death; but this mysterious growth from an unreckoned Past multiplies with every year and argues immortality. Men may die, empires dissolve and time change the face of the world itself, but this wondrous tree, before which from time out of mind the Hindoo has knelt in prayer, proves to him its divinity by its constant, silent, certain triumphs over all the years. The lightning is a plaything for the mighty grove, the hurricane a welcome refreshment, and the very earthquake but quickens its roots.

Every column of this verdant temple is alive, and the passing seasons witness its increment of girth and power. "The trees of the Lord are full of sap." The apothecaries' art has turned its products into medicine, and "the leaves of the tree are for the healing of the nations." Is not this vision of beauty, this tent for an army, this retreat for the unfallen sparrow, this laden table spread in the wilderness for the lowly families of animated nature, this Tree of Life, a shadow of the church? "Behold," said Jesus, "the fig tree!"

In the story of this church's visible life we shall find an example of the force of the Kingdom of God in human hearts bearing fruit, through His grace, in multitudes of regenerated human lives.

The past of the Reformed Dutch Church of Greenbush ("Greene-Bos") is interwoven with the whole history of this region. In A. D. 1652—one hundred and thirty-five years previous to the organization of this church, and one hundred and forty years before the township was created—*Gerrit Smith* was commissioned from the church in Holland to perform ministerial duties here. Nor was he the first. His commission reads: "He shall use for his dwelling the house formerly used by the former preacher, situated in Greenbush, and there reside with his family and exercise his aforesaid office ("Schout") with all due diligence and fidelity, according to the laws, edicts and ordinances already or to be enacted there. * * * Having arrived, with God's help, at the island of Manhattan, he shall proceed by the first opportunity to the colony and report himself to Jan Baptist Van Rensselaer and make known to him his quality by exhibition of his commission and instructions. He shall above all things take care that divine worship shall be maintained in said colony conformably to the Reformed religion in this country, as the same is publicly taught in these United Provinces. He shall in like manner pay attention that the Lord's Day, the Sabbath of the New Testament, be properly respected, both by the observance of hearing the Holy Word as well as the preventing all unnecessary and daily labor on that day. And whereas, it is a scandal that the Christians should mingle themselves unlawfully with the wives or daughters of the heathen, the officer shall labor to put in execution the placards and ordinances enacted or to be enacted against the same, and strictly exact the fines imposed hereby without any dissimulation."

He was to receive for his services one hundred and fifty dollars, all fines and penalties amounting to ten guilders, or under, and one-third of all in excess of that amount.*

The province was known as Rensselaerwyck, and

---

* Sylvester's History of Rensselaer County.

its settlement was coeval with that of Beaverwyck, or Albany. It is believed that divine worship was held in "Greene Bos" as early as at any point north of Manhattan Island. The land on this side the river was so superior to that on the west that patroon Van Rensselaer encouraged the earlier settlements here. He was a strong adherent of the Church of Holland, and as we have seen, the minister sent from the Netherlands was accredited to him. There is an authentic old record to the purport that timber for a church edifice was sent from Holland to Greenbush several years before the first church was erected at Albany. For some unknown reason the design was not carried out, and the timber was used in the construction of "an old-fashioned low-eaved barn of sixty by seventy feet dimensions, which was consumed in a great fire in the village."* The church was to have been built on *Douw's Point*, within the limits of East Greenbush, and would have taken the place of the room, whatever it was, in which public worship had been held from the beginning.

So this territory on which we stand is not only among the earliest occupied by white men on the American Continent as their home, but probably antedates all other places, except Jamestown, Plymouth and Manhattan, in stated Christian worship. Just as the council fires of the Mohicans died out, another fire was kindled on this spot, which for two hundred and fifty years has gladdened the eyes and warmed the hearts of thousands, and has drawn us together to-day.

It is also matter for gratitude and honest pride that this land on which we were born and on which our churches are builded, was not stolen from the aborigines, nor seized as the spoils of unjust warfare, but was bought and paid for by Mr. Van Rensselaer before he set up his manorial title. The Mohican chief, Narranemit, conveyed for a price by regular deed, signed with his own hand, his grounds called "Semessick," and which included Greenbush. This was followed a few years later by his purchase of all the lands back into the interior claimed by the Indian grantors, and with his previous purchase he thus became proprietor of a tract of country twenty-four by forty-eight miles in extent, containing some seven hundred thousand acres, now comprising the counties of Albany and Rensselaer, and a portion of Columbia.

But though with old Dutch honesty the territory had been purchased of the occupying tribe of Mohicans, other red men of the woods were found to dispute with the settlers pre-emptive rights, and much of this land was purchased of different Indian claimants several times over. Alarms were not infrequent, and no house was safe without weapons of defence. The soil in this region was so wonderfully favorable to the production of Indian corn, that the savages were reluctant to give it up. The most famous of many rich tracts was the cornfield on the Evert O. Lansing farm. On one occasion several men returning from the cornfield to the old "Bomb Barrack"—still standing and occupied, two hundred and fifty years old, on Staats' Island—were waylaid by savages near the David Rector place, a couple of miles from this spot. Several were killed and others wounded. In 1777 a man from Scott's Corners, named Shans, had started for Albany with a load of wheat, accompanied by a negro. They were set on by Indians and both were killed and scalped. The frightened horses ran to the residence of Mr. Lansing, thus conveying the dreadful news.

There are many such traditions of those days, and it is little wonder that the stern old settlers deemed the life of a hostile Indian forfeited on sight. There is a story of a brave old believer in fore-ordination, that when starting out to go to another settlement—Scott's Corners or Nassau, perhaps—he carefully prepared his gun and ammunition for the journey. His grown-up boys, thinking to make a point against their father, rallied him on his precautions. "No matter about the gun, father," they said; "you know you won't die till your time comes!" "Yes, yes I know that," said the sharp old man, "but suppose I should leave my gun at home and then meet an Indian in the woods yonder, and *his* time had come, what then?" If the savages ever imagined they could frighten a Dutchman off from land he had bought and paid for, their delusion cost them dear.

The tribe of the Mohicans claimed that theirs was among the most ancient of all aboriginal nations. "One of their traditions was to the purport that many many moons before the white man came, their ancestors had lived in a far-off country to the west, beyond the mighty rivers and mountains, at a place where the waters constantly moved to and fro, and that, in the belief that there existed away toward the rising sun a red man's paradise—a land of deer and salmon and beaver—they had traveled on towards the east and south to find it, but that they were scourged and divided by famine, so that it was not until after long and weary journeyings they came at length to this broad and beautiful river which forever ebbed and flowed like the waters from which they had come; and that here amidst a profusion of game and fish they rested, and found that Indian elysium of which they dreamed before they left their old homes in the land of the setting sun."*

---

* Sylvester's History of Rensselaer County.

This plausible legend may never be verified, but it is none the less true that this land of the Mohicans was a spot of rare fertility. They reared immense crops of corn, and this cereal which will always bear the Indian name, seems to have furnished them with the larger part of their food supplies. A shoulder-blade of the moose or deer, or a clam-shell rudely fastened to a stick, was the implement of agriculture, and as a fertilizer a fish was buried in each hill of corn. The words hominy and succotash are of Indian origin.

The entire work of planting and harvesting the crop was done by women, the men reserving to themselves the raising of tobacco as too sacred for women to use or handle.

Not only the field, but forest and flood yielded generous supplies. The river and stream abounded with fish, and the moose and deer, beaver, bear, wild turkey, pigeon and partridge, nuts, berries and roots furnished exhaustless luxuries with little toil.

The first name given by white men to this territory we call Greenbush was *De Laet's Burg*, so called in honor of the historian of Hendrick Hudson's expedition up the river in September, 1609. Hudson anchored on the eighteenth of that month at a point opposite the present site of Castleton, according to his own account. He came ashore, and the famous navigator was probably the first white man to set foot upon this soil. The historian, De Laet, gives the following interesting extract from Hudson's journal of the incident:

"I sailed to the shore in one of their canoes with an old man who was chief of a tribe consisting of forty men and seventeen women. These I saw there in a house well constructed of oak bark and circular in shape, so that it had the appearance of being built with an arched roof. It contained a great quantity of Indian corn and beans of the last year's growth, and there lay near the house, for the purpose of drying, enough to load three ships, beside what was growing in the fields. On our coming into the house two mats were spread out to sit upon, and some food was immediately served in well-made red wooden bowls. Two men were also despatched at once with bows and arrows in quest of game, who soon brought in a pair of pigeons which they had shot. They likewise killed a fat dog and skinned it in great haste with shells which they had got out of the water. They supposed that I would remain with them for the night, but I returned after a short time on board the ship. The land is the finest for cultivation that I ever in my life set foot upon, and it also abounds in trees of every description. These natives are a very good people, for when they saw that I would not remain with them they supposed that I was afraid of their bows, and taking their arrows they broke them in pieces and threw them into the fire."

This was in Greenbush, about two miles from this spot, and about three hundred years ago.

The navigator who thus becomes related to us in an interesting way, continued up the river in his ship, the *Half Moon*, to the head of tide-water, as is supposed, near where the Mohawk empties into the Hudson. He named the river with a fitness better than he knew—*The River of the Mountains.*

In his brief history of East Greenbush, Mr. Sylvester gives the following description from "Dwight's Travels in 1798," showing that Hudson's estimate of its great fertility was justified in the lapse of time, and affording an interesting glimpse into the ways of our forefathers:

"After crossing the ferry at Albany, we rode over a charming interval at Greenbush, handsomer and more fertile than any I had seen on this road. It extends several miles toward the south and is divided into beautiful farms and planted in a thin dispersion with houses and outbuildings, whose appearance sufficiently indicated the easy circumstances of their proprietors. From the excellent gardens which I have at times seen in this spot and the congeniality of the soil to every hortulan production of this climate, I should naturally have believed that the inhabitants would have supplied the people of Albany with vegetables. Instead of this, they are principally furnished by the Shakers of New Lebanon,—a strong proof of the extreme reluctance with which the Dutch farmers quit their ancient customs, even when allured by the prospects of superior gain."

From the old records in the office of the Patroon, it appears that this little village, now called East Greenbush, was settled as early as 1630. No documents or legends of its founding are known to exist, and the ancient date alone survives to remind us that more than a quarter of a millennium has passed since white men first climbed this healthful hill to build, to plant, and, let us believe, to pray.

But one hundred years ago this ground was the scene of notable events. The wilderness had blossomed. A plain structure of forty or forty-five feet square, with gambrel roof fronting the north, and with main entrance on the east side, had been erected the year before, and was now filled with substantial-looking men and women, bearing an aspect of unwonted and earnest interest. A passing Indian might have wondered at the sight, and indeed a pale-faced stranger would have fain paused to inquire, What did it all mean? The people needed houses to dwell in, and shelter for harvest and herd. But this building is neither dwelling nor barn. Nothing like it was ever seen in the region before. Let us enter and look and listen. A man of reverend aspect, fifty years of age, is standing in an elevated inclosure, speaking. It is Dr. Eilardus Westerlo, for thirty years pastor of the First Reformed Dutch Church of Albany, and he is giving a name to the edifice. He calls it a "House of Prayer," and says in subdued tones, as if he felt the Unseen Presence, "Let us pray!" Every head is bowed in worship as the venerable man invokes a benediction, offers thanks for the providence that has crowned the building enterprise, implores that wisdom may be given to the people in their purpose to establish here a new church of Christ, and prays for its future prosperity. We and our fathers and our children were included in that prayer, precious answers to which the heavens have now been shedding upon three generations.

And the time was auspicious. It was four years after the close of the Revolutionary war and the treaty of peace with Great Britain, and John Adams had been accredited to England as ambassador from the United States of America. Three days after this church was organized, the American Federal Constitution was adopted at Philadelphia, and peace and hope reigned everywhere. The thirty years' war of "Coetus" and "Conferentie" in the Reformed Protestant Dutch Church in

America, on the question of education and ordination of ministers in Holland or here—a controversy which "Old Colony" Zabriskie designates as the "Guelph and Ghibeline war of our church"—a controversy which was so sharp that it alienated very friends and divided families, and so prolonged that it threatened ultimate ruin—had been amicably settled by the consent of the mother church in Holland to the independence of that in America. It was sixty-seven years after the incorporation of the Reformed Protestant Dutch Church of America by King George the First, and five years after the commencement of preaching in English in Albany —"a half day each Sabbath." But it was ten years before the building of the North Dutch Church on Pearl street, fourteen years before the "Albany and Boston turnpike" was laid out, forty-three years before the "Greenbush and Schodack Academy" was built, and five years before Greenbush was organized into a town.

It is greatly to be regretted that the records of our churches are so generally incomplete. During a few of your pastorates the journals were scrupulously kept, but of others scarcely a page of history remains.

And it has also seemed to be specially unfortunate that since this celebration was finally resolved on, the church had been closed for extensive repairs, with no meeting of the congregation for nearly three months. With a scattered flock, without a shepherd, little could be done to supplement imperfect records by those vivid traditions born of courage, of sacrifice, of zeal and devotion, of joy and triumph, which, when left to unwritten history, are so often left to die. A pastor mingling with the people might have chronicled many an incident which drew a tear, evoked a prayer or inspired a song in this dear old church, which it has been impossible for your historian in his limited time to procure. But it is matter for devout thankfulness to our fathers' God that in the flying years, and frequent pastoral changes, so much of authentic history remains. And the historian trusts that, though like the books of the Apocrypha, his story is uninspired, yet like those writings it may be accounted useful as history. "*And if I have done well, and as is fitting the story, it is that which I desired: but if slenderly and meanly, it is that which I could attain to.*"—*II. Maccabees, XV.* 38.

ORGANIZATION.

The "Reformed Protestant Low Dutch Church of Greene-Bos, in the manor of Rensselaerwyck and county of Albany," was organized in the "newly-built House of Prayer," on the fourteenth day of September, in the year of our Lord one thousand seven hundred and eighty-seven, by enrollment of the following membership:

Harmon Van Hoesen,
Yachem Staats,
Peter M. Van Buren,
Jonathan Witbeck,
Barent C. Van Buren,
Benjamin Van De Berg,
Christopher Yates *en vrouw*, Catrina Lansingh,
Kasparus Witbeck,
John Lansing,
Abraham Cooper,
Jacob Ostrander,
Gerard Ostrander,
Thomas Mesick *en vrouw*, Maria Wiesener,
Melchert Vanderpool,
George Shordenbergh,
Matthew Shordenbergh,
Abraham Ostrander *en vrouw*, Elizabeth Ostrander,
Petrus Ham,
John Muller *en vrouw*.

The edifice had been erected in the previous year upon this spot, which is four miles southeast of the city of Albany, and two miles distant from the Hudson river, on a highway afterwards known as the Albany and Boston Turnpike.

The record of the meeting is in the Holland language and is very beautifully written. It is our most important document to-day and must be given entire. Here is the translation:

"'The persons who have anxiously made their request of the Consistory of the Reformed Dutch Church of Albany, to the end that a Reformed Dutch Church might be organized in this place for which to elect a Consistory, have for this purpose been called to meet together to-day, and did meet in the newly-built house of prayer, when Rev. Dr. Westerlo, after calling upon God's name, made a short address to the people and earnestly requested all the male members who were present, that they should elect from among them, in the presence of the whole congregation, three Elders and three Deacons. Accordingly the following persons were unanimously elected:

Peter M. Van Buren,	Abraham Cooper,
Abraham Ostrander,	John E. Lansing,
Christopher Yates,	Casparus Witbeck,
Elders.	*Deacons.*

"The which were presented before the congregation to learn if they had any objection why these persons should not be lawfully ordained, and no objection being made, these persons were accordingly ordained to their respective offices, after which the whole congregation, having with one accord invoked God's blessing upon the further upbuilding of their society, were dismissed.

"Whereupon the newly-ordained Consistory unitedly concluded to keep themselves by the constitution of the Reformed Dutch Church in the Synod of Dort, in the years 1618 and '19, bound in union with the Christian synod of the Dutch churches in the States of New York and New Jersey, and belonging to the Classis of Albany.

"There was also present with us Mr. Henry Schermerhorn, an Elder of Schodack, saying that other members of their Consistory were hindered from coming here with him for the purpose, if possible, to unite themselves with this society in the calling of one pastor for both societies. Upon which the Consistory of Greenbush proceeded to send a call to Dr. Peter Lowe as shepherd and pastor of this society, to attend to the service of the Lord every other Lord's day for the yearly income of £80.

"The aforesaid Elder certified that the Consistory of the society of Schodack had resolved on their part to furnish the half of the salary, with a dwelling for the minister at Schodack, or wherever his honor might choose, with the necessary fuel.

"Upon which the Rev. Mr. Westerlo was requested to write out a call, and also to state that for further emergency, they would on each New

Year's day make him a present of £10, each society giving £5.

"The limits of this congregation, to distinguish it from that of Schodack, are the house of Jonathan Witbeck at the river, and from there to the house of Casparus Lodewick, and as far north as the commonly-called *Jan Vorms padt;* and that any who lived within the aforesaid limits, and who belonged to the church in Albany could, if they so desired, remain in that church as long as they thought it best to do so."

So much was done the first day. The next record is as follows:

"January, 1788. As Mr. Lowe did not accept the aforesaid call, we, the Consistory of this society, with those of Schodack, have extended a call upon Dr. Jacobus Van Campen Romeyn, which was as follows:

"'The Rev. Jacobus Van Campen Romeyn, S. S. Ministerial Candidate. We, the undersigned, Elders and Deacons of the Low Dutch Reformed Societies of Schodack and Greenbush, in the State of New York, together united and in the fear of God, have met together and have unanimously concluded to extend to your honour, as you will see by the opening of this signed and sealed letter, our choice of you to be the Ordinary shepherd and teacher of the two afore-mentioned communities for the honour of God and our mutual benefit, so that your honour will be obliged to preach to us twice each Lord's day, once in the Dutch and once in the English language, by turns to the different communities; and afternoons as customary to preach from the Heidelbergh Catechism, and also upon the feast days to administer the Holy Sacraments, to work for the welfare of the church, to catechise the young, and to perform all things according to the Requirements of a faithful minister of the Gospel, according to the Rule of the Dutch Reformed Church in the Synod of Dort, in the years 1618 and '19, confirmed and united with the Christian Synod of the Reformed Dutch Churches in the States of New York and New Jersey. For which services faithfully discharged, we, the undersigned, Elders and Deacons, each for our respective societies, promise, and also our successors promise, and bind ourselves to pay to your honour yearly, and that in two equal parts, the full salary amount of one hundred and fifty pounds in legal coin of the State of New York, each society to pay the sum of seventy-five pounds, and also to furnish a Respectable Residence at Schodack or wheresoever your honour might choose, with its privileges.

"'May the Lord who alone is good persuade your honour to follow in His fear upon this our Call, and come over to us in the full blessing of the Gospel.

"'Written, signed and sealed this Day. Nov. 28th, 1787.

And'w. Ten Eyck,   Peter M. Van Buren,
Jacobus V. D. Pool,   Abraham Ostrander,
John H. Beekman,   Chris'r. Yates,
Jacob C. Schermerhorn,   Abraham Cooper,
Roelef Jansen,   Casparus Witbeck,
Dan'l. Schermerhorn,   John E. Lansing,
Maus Van Buren,   *Von Greenbush.*
      Von Schodack.'

"Upon the first day of May, 1788, it pleased the Lord to persuade the afore-mentioned teacher to accept the call of the afore-mentioned societies and come over to them, and he was ordained and installed on the fifteenth day of June, in the church of Greenbush, by the Rev. Dr. Dr. Dr. Thomas Romeyn, Dirk Romeyn and Eilardus Westerlo, the sermon being delivered by Dr. D. Romeyn, from Col. IV. 17: '*And say to Archippus, Take heed to the ministry which thou hast received in the Lord, that thou fulfil it.*'

"The aforesaid call was accepted with the following additions:

"1. While it is customary in the Low Dutch Reformed Church to allow the minister some Sundays on which he may vacate himself and have for his own, and the said call not mentioning any, we, the ordained Consistory, grant that whenever their minister thought it necessary to be absent from his people, he was at liberty to do so.

"2. The Consistory also resolved and promised that in addition to the afore-mentioned salary they would furnish for their minister pasture for his stock.

"As the selection of a residence was left to the choice of their minister, so his honour chose to reside at Schodack; accordingly the Consistory of Schodack took upon themselves the necessary preparation of the dwelling and paying all the expenses of the same without the help of the society of Greenbush."

The last chronicle of this notable first year relates to the methods adopted for revenue, and shows that the spirit of harmony and brotherhood reigned in the church.

"1788. In Consistory. Present: Jacobus Van Campen Romeyn, V. D. M.

Elders.	*Deacons.*
Abraham Ostrander,	John E. Lansing.
Peter M. Van Buren,	Abraham Cooper,
Chris'r. Yates,	Casparus Witbeck.

"DISPOSING OF SEATS.

"1. As the house of worship being erected is now finished, the Consistory thought it proper that the seats should be sold.

"2. That the money proceeding from this sale should be applied toward paying off the debt made by the building of the church..

"3. That each seat should be taxed with the yearly rental of three shillings, and that the above-named rent should be merged in the subscription list for salary; of course as much as any should be indebted for their rent, it would be discounted from the Subscription list, and if the rent should exceed his subscription, he is required to pay the full amount of said seat and be discharged from his subscription.

"4. And that in case a seat should be sold or transferred over to another by an occupant, it should be signed over to the buyer, for the registering of which he would be required to pay the amount of four shillings to the Consistory.

"5. That notice should be given from the pulpit about the foregoing resolutions three Sundays previously, and the time for the sale should be fixed upon Wednesday, at which time the conditions would be made known to all who should be present.

"And after rendering thanks to God, the whole assembly took leave, one of the other, in Peace and Love. J. P. JACOBUS ROMEYN."

(In a subsequent note dated "Wednesday, 1788," it is said that the sale was held according to the above resolutions, and that the minister was "requested to make a register of the seats sold and to write them down in the Church Book." This "register" has not been preserved).

Another event of historic importance occurred this year. On the twelfth of August the church was duly incorporated under the statute, six days previous to the incorporation of the older church of Schodack. The title assumed was: "The Minister, Elders and Deacons of the Reformed Protestant Dutch Church of Greenbush, in the County of Albany." This was ratified by record in the office of the County Clerk of the county of Albany on September 12th of the same year. (The title was altered by act of the Legislature February 7th, 1807, to: "The Reformed Protestant Dutch Congregation of Greenbush, in the County of Rensselaer.")

Copy of record in book entitled "Church Patents No. 1."

"23. Whereas, by virtue of an Act entitled 'An Act making such alterations in the Act for incorporating religious societies as to render the same more convenient to the Reformed Protestant Dutch Congregations, passed the 7th day of March, 1788, we, the subscribers, Jacobus Vc. Romeyn, *Minister*, Christopher Yates, Abraham Ostrander and Peter M. Van Buren, *Elders*, and Abraham Cooper, Kasparus Witbeck and John E. Lansing, *Deacons*, of the Reformed Protestant Dutch Church or Congregation lately formed and established at Greenbush, in the county of Albany, having assembled together at the said church on this 12th day of August,

1788, by virtue of the said Act, do by these presents certify that the trustees of the said Church or Congregation and their successors forever, shall as a body corporate be called, distinguished and known by the style and title of the Minister, Elders and Deacons of the Reformed Protestant Dutch Church, of Greenbush, in the county of Albany. In witness whereof, we, the said Minister, Elders and Deacons have hereunto set our hands and seals the day and year last above written.

      JACOBUS VC. ROMEYN, [L.S.]
      CHRISTOPHER YATES, [L.S.]
      ABRAHAM OSTRANDER, [L.S.]
      PETER M. VAN BUREN, [L.S.]
      ABRAHAM COOPER, [L.S.]
         his
      KASPARUS X WITBECK, [L.S.]
        mark.
      JOHN E. LANSING. [L.S.]

Signed and sealed
in the presence of us,
 ANTHONY BREES,
 JAS. MCKOWN.

"Be it remembered, that on the 12th day of September, in the year of our Lord one thousand seven hundred and eighty-eight, personally appeared before me, John M. Beekman, Esquire, one of the judges of the Court of Common Pleas for the city and county of Albany, Anthony Brees, one of the subscribing witnesses to the within instrument, who, being duly sworn, says that he saw Jacob. Vc. Romeyn, Christopher Yates, Abraham Ostrander, Abraham Cooper, Casparus Witbeck and John E. Lansing, sign, seal and deliver the within instrument for the uses and purposes therein mentioned, and that he, this deponent, together with James McKown, respectively, subscribed their names thereto as witnesses; and I, having perused the same and finding therein no erasures, interlineations or obliterations, do allow the same to be recorded.

JOHN M. BEEKMAN."

In the same book of "Church Patents" is the record of Incorporation of the Reformed Protestant Dutch Church of Schodack, on the 18th of August, 1788, signed, sealed and attested as follows:

"JAC. VC. ROMEYN, [L.S.]
ANDRUS TEN EYCK, [L.S.]
JOHN H. BEEKMAN, [L.S.]
JACOB C. SCHERMERHORN, [L.S.]
JACOBUS VANDER POOL, [L.S.]
DANIEL SCHERMERHORN, [L.S.]
JOHN J. VAN VOLKENBURGH, [L.S.]
MAES VAN BUREN, [L.S.]
ROELEF JOHNSON, [L.S.]"

"Signed and sealed
in the presence of us,

ANTHONY TEN EYCK,
CORNS. SCHERMERHORN.

ALTERING OF CORPORATE NAME.

The organization of the County of Rensselaer in 1791, and some ecclesiastical changes also, made it desirable to alter the title of church corporation. This was done in the twentieth year of its history.

LAWS OF NEW YORK, A. D. 1807.

Passed the 30th Session, 1807.

MORGAN LEWIS, ESQUIRE, Governor.

(Copied in office of Secretary of State, Sept. 21st, A. D. 1887, from volume entitled "Printed copy of the Laws, 24.")

"CHAPTER III.

"An act to alter the name of the incorporation of the Dutch congregation of Greenbush, in the county of Rensselaer.

(Preamble stating that the name of the incorporation has become inapplicable):

"Whereas, the minister, elders and deacons of the Dutch congregation of Greenbush, in the county of Rensselaer, have, by their petition to the legislature, stated that their said congregation was incorporated agreeable to the directions of an act entitled, 'An act making such alterations in the act for incorporating religious societies, as to render the same more convenient to the reformed protestant Dutch congregations, passed the seventh day of March, one thousand seven hundred and eighty-eight,' and that the said incorporation took place at the time when the said town of Greenbush formed a part of the county of Albany, and that they assumed the name of the minister, elders and deacons of the reformed protestant Dutch church of Greenbush, in the county of Albany; therefore,

"Be it enacted by the people of the state of New York, represented in senate and assembly, That the said congregation shall hereafter be distinguished and known by the name of 'the reformed protestant Dutch congregation of Greenbush, in the county of Rensselaer.'

"STATE OF NEW YORK.

In Assembly, February 7th, 1807.
This bill having been read the third time—
Resolved, That the bill do pass.
By order of the Assembly,

A. M. CARD, Speaker.

"STATE OF NEW YORK.

In Senate, February 10th, 1807.
This bill having been read the third time—
Resolved, That the bill do pass.
By order of the Senate,

JNO. BROOME, Presid't.

"IN COUNCIL OF REVISION.

February the 20th, 1807.

Resolved, That it does not appear improper to the council that this bill should become a law of this state. MORGAN LEWIS."

One hundred years, 1,200 months, 5,200 weeks, 36,500 days, 876,000 hours, 52,560,000 minutes, 3,153,600,000 heart-beats! This is a century in simple outline, but who can begin to tell the sum of the life of a christian church for a hundred years?

Brethren, in this period the Divine Master has sent you twelve apostles, with an average pastorate of one hundred months. Ten of them are dead—as much as such men can die—and one of the survivors has been touched by the beckoning finger of God. To eight of the number this was their first pastorate, whose ages at installation averaged about twenty-three years. To two others this was their fourth charge; to one the fifth, and to one the seventh, and it is believed that none of the twelve had reached the age of twenty-four years at the time of his ordination. The shortest pastoral term was two and a half years, and the longest seventeen and a half. Of the ten deceased, their average natural life was sixty-eight years, and that of their ministerial life forty-five years. None

J. V. C. ROMEYN.
From Oil Painting in Chapel of Rutgers College.

have died here; but the baby dust of a child of Dr. Marselus, and one of Dr. Liddell lies under the shadow of this sanctuary.

THE FIRST PASTOR.
1788-1799.

Jacobus Van Campen Romeyn was called Nov. 28th, 1787, and dismissed to accept a call to the church of Hackensack, N. J., in the spring or summer of 1799. He served the latter church thirty-five years, when he was stricken with partial paralysis and soon afterward resigned his charge. He halted upon his thigh for eight years and then fell asleep.

He was a son of Rev. Thomas Romeyn, who, with his brother Theodoric, was the first of a line of ministers whose names are justly household words of pride in the Reformed Dutch Church of America. Here is the list by direct male descent: Thomas, James Van Campen, James and Theodore B.; while the Taylors, Zabriskies, Danforths and Berrys, and I know not how many to whom their daughters transmitted faith like an heir-loom, adorn just as brightly the history of our Zion.

His wife, Susan Van Vranken, was born at Schenectady Feb. 9th, 1771. They were married May 29th, 1788, just after his installation, when he was in his twenty-third and she in her eighteenth year.

In their family Bible, now in the possession of their grandson, Rev. F. N. Zabriskie, of Princeton, N. J., is the following record:

Children Born.

Susan Van Campen,	February 6th, 1790.
Harriet,	June 19th, 1792.
Maria,	October 23d, 1794.
James,	September 30th, 1797.
Anna,	May 11th, 1800.
Elizabeth,	July 3d, 1802.
Caroline,	December 10th, 1807.
Thos. Theodore,	August 22d, 1810.
Sarah,	February 22d, 1813.

None of these children are now living. Four of them were born during Mr. Romeyn's ministry here—Susan, Harriet, Maria and James. Of this James, Dr. Corwin, author of the "*Manual of the Reformed Church in America,*" says he became "perhaps the most eloquent of our preachers—a flame of fire in the pulpit." Anna, the fifth child, was the wife of your fifth pastor, Rev. B. C. Taylor, and the mother and grandmother of ministers.

The joy expressed by the Consistory that the Lord had "persuaded" this man to listen to their call, was amply justified in the sequel. For in that early day, and during his ministry of eleven years, one hundred and eighty-five persons were added to this church alone. The church books of Schodack, where he also served, are lost, and those of Wynantskill, where he preached the remaining five years, are either lost or are inaccessible. If anything like a similar prosperity prevailed in those communities—which seems probable, for in six years Schodack was erected into a separate charge—it would show that his labor here was not only the most fruitful this region has ever known, but also one of the most remarkable in the whole denominational annals. Early in his pastorate the church found it necessary to increase the number of elders and deacons to the full constitutional limit, to meet the growing wants of the congregation. His watchful eye must have been upon every man, woman and child in his whole parish, and he left no means unemployed to win them to the service of his Master. No one now living in this congregation can remember his ministry here, which terminated eighty-eight years ago, but the fruit of it is all around us. He wrote, with a beautiful hand, the first records of this church—your book of Genesis—and his personal piety and fruitful life show that, like his Master, he "was in the beginning with God." The first of the twelve apostles whom the Lord has sent you, he was a magnate fit to lead the noble procession. His veins were full of the blood of the prophets. His father, three uncles, three of his six brothers and his son, gave themselves to the work of the ministry, and his children's children have caught the banners from their sires' failing hands, one of whom—Rev. James Romeyn Berry—has to-day been permitted to unfurl it again on the outmost wall of this citadel sanctuary of a hundred years. It is a royal priesthood race, a peculiar people, and their family emblem should be an altar smoking with incense in a temple whose lamps never go out.

The records say that, though he was disposed to remain here, yet he accepted an urgent call to Hackensack, where his ministry extended from 1799 to 1833. "It fell," says Dr. Berry, "upon the most troublous times in our denomination in this section of the country. Previous to his call to the church the signs of a fearful tempest were thickening on every hand. Hackensack already gave tokens of becoming the principal point of the great struggle which ensued. The great need was a man who should properly combine the elements of true piety, firmness, prudence and love of peace. These characteristics Mr. Romeyn was widely known to possess, and upon the basis of this reputation he was called to the pastorate of the churches of Hackensack and Schraalenburgh, without having been heard or seen among them. * * * Of his piety the sweetest memories have been cherished by those who knew him in the fond relations of his home, or in the confidence of personal friendship. His natural loving and sincere disposition was sanctified by his sincere and loving faith in Jesus. This gave his children that peculiar fondness with which they regarded him while living and revered his memory when dead." Rev. Herman Van Derwart, his latest successor in the Hackensack church, says that Mr. Romeyn's pastorate was "the longest in the two hundred years of the church's history."

It was my privilege one day last month to copy from his family Bible at Princeton this tender tribute from his pen:

"Susan, my beloved wife, and the mother of the children recorded in the adjoining column, deceased of dropsy in the chest, April 22d, 1826, at fifteen minutes past three in the morning. She fell asleep in Jesus, with a hope full of immortality."

"One day in August, 1832," says another grandson, Rev. Benjamin C. Taylor, "while sitting at his own table he was suddenly stricken with paralysis. He silently burst into tears, and received the stroke as a signal that his work was nearly done. As this attack was comparatively slight, he somewhat recovered from it and resumed his pulpit labor, and with great effort continued to serve at God's altar. But his work was done and well done." "It is doubtful," says Dr. Berry, "if the whole number of

[7]

the ministers of our church in that day could have furnished another who would have borne the trials and met the difficulties of his position better than he."

His last public service was a funeral sermon in the Dutch language over one of the most aged members of his church. In his last address at the Communion table, enfeebled by paralysis, and with broken utterance, he began his remarks in the affecting language of Job—" Have pity upon me, O ye my friends, for the hand of God hath touched me!"

During the last eight years of his life the earthly house of his tabernacle was shattered by repeated attacks of paralysis. His mind suffered in the feebleness of his body. Patiently he awaited the signal for his departure. The last token of earthly recognition was given in response to the question: "Do you know that you are almost home?" In a few hours that home was reached and mortality was swallowed up of life. He died on the 27th day of June, 1840, in the seventy-fifth year of his age. His ashes repose in the cemetery at Hackensack, and his tombstone bears this legend:

"In memory of Rev. James V. C. Romeyn, who died June 27th, 1840, in the seventy-fifth year of his age and fifty-third of his ministry, having served the united congregations of Hackensack and Schraalenbergh thirty-five years.

"I have waited for thy salvation, O God."

JOHN LANSING ZABRISKIE.
TAKEN BEFORE MARRIAGE.

He was honored by the church with a trusteeship of Queen's College, and as president of Classis, and like his great namesake, the apostle James, president of the college at Jerusalem, was worthy of all honor.

I have lingered thus long and lovingly around this name partly because he was your first annointed teacher, partly because he was so grand and good, and partly because the materials for biography are so ample. I have scarcely opened them; but duty to the occasion forbids indulgence in the grateful task.

II.

REV. JOHN LANSING ZABRISKIE.

1801–1811.

After an interval of about one year, Rev. John Lansing Zabriskie was ordained and installed. He was born at Albany in 1779, graduated at Union College in 1797, studied theology under Dr. Dirck Romeyn, and was licensed to preach by the Classis of Albany in the year 1800. Like Mr. Romeyn, he served this church ten years, when he accepted a call to Millstone (Hillsborough), N. J., where he preached for thirty-nine years, dying in 1850, aged seventy-one. His call to this church was approved by Classis August 19th, 1800. Greenbush and Wynantskill were his charges, and the parsonage was at Blooming Grove. His first record is of the baptism of two infants on February 15th, 1801— Henry Smith, born December 25th, 1800, and Peter Breesey, born October 30th, 1800.

The church records, which, unfortunately, are very incomplete, show an addition during his ministry of forty-eight members to the Greenbush portion of his pastoral charge. There are a few persons yet lingering here who remember him as the minister of their childhood.

On the first page of the first account book in the archives of this church appears this entry:

"Received from the Consistory of Greenbush by the hands of Peter Whitaker the sum of One Hundred and thirty-three dollars and twenty-five cents.

August 17th, 1801. JOHN L. ZABRISKIE."

An interesting item of history is written near the close of his ministry here:

"The Consistory having taken into their serious consideration, so far as it relates to the preaching in the Dutch language, and feeling inclined to accommodate such Persons belonging to the church who do not understand Dutch and who are no way benefited when the service is performed in that language—considering also the general Prevalence of the English Language, and the daily desire of the Dutch, are induced to Resolve as follows:

"Resolved unanimously, that the service in this

church shall in future be two-thirds in the English Language and one-third in the Dutch.

"And also Resolved that the Rev. Mr. Zabriskie Publish this Resolution to the Congregation."

Here is also an interesting item :

"30th June, 1806, received of the consistory of Greenbush by the hands of John Ostrander, Deacon, the sum of Three Dollars, in full for one year's salary as sexton of said church.

$3.   ADAM COOK.

In October, 1810, Mr. Zabriskie applied to Classis for release from the charge. Both the Consistories—Greenbush and Wynantskill—refused to unite with him in the request, and Classis denied it at first, but on the next day, October 17th, reconsidered their action and dissolved the relation. At a meeting held in Greenbush February 19th, 1811, the two congregations sent in a remonstrance against the action and prayed for its reconsideration. The Classis endeavored to secure the release of Mr. Zabriskie from the church of Millstone, to which he had accepted a call, but failed.*

Rev. Dr. Abram Messler, in an appreciative biographical account, says of him : "During his long pastorate at Millstone he maintained his influence and his standing to the end. All who knew

---

* Rensselaer Classis Records..

him loved him, and those who knew him best esteemed him most.

"He was one of the most laborious and successful pastors in Somerset county. He preached and lectured more, visited more families and attended more carefully to all his public duties than almost any other pastor of his time. He was considered by all not only an *example*, but a *monitor* in his official life. He was an excellent preacher, and though he seldom wrote his sermons, they were solid, sensible, full of evangelical thought, and listened to with profit by all the earnest-hearted and godly of his congregations. Few men could speak more judiciously and appropriately from the impulse of the moment on any given theme.

"His life was unstained by even a breath of evil. In a word, he was a good man, useful in his day, and he has left a name which will have a savor of excellence for many generations among those whose fathers and mothers he led in the way of life."

NOTE.—Rev. John L. Zabriskie was a judicious, sensible, wise man; an excellent "old-fashioned" preacher. He was in person short and stout, with a large head and face, genial in expression, and easy in manners. With all his habitual gravity and professional air, at times in his social intercourse he would astonish and excite you by his wit, his sarcasm, and even drollery. He knew the Gospel, and felt it, and preached it with clearness, zeal, and often with great power of immediate impression.—(W. J. R. T.)

NOTE.—"One of the most Nathaniel-like men was John L. Jabriskie. He was eminently a man of peace, and of great simplicity of character. Without any pretensions to greatness, his ministry was truly evangelical, and he saw the children and the children's children come into the church. His house was the much-loved place of ministerial meeting."—(Rev. Isaac Ferris, D.D.)

NOTE.—Quite near the entrance of the Millstone Church stands an imposing monument of marble with the following inscription on its eastern front:

In memory of
The Reverend John Lansing Zabriskie.
Born March 4, 1779.
Died August 15, 1850.

For more than 50 years a minister of God. From 1811 until his death Pastor of the Dutch Reformed Church at Millstone.

Pure in life, sincere in purpose, with zeal, perseverance and prudence, devoted to the service of his Master, here, amid the loved people of his charge, his earthly remains await the resurrection of the just.—(P. T. P.)

III.

REV. ISAAC LABAGH.
1811–1814.

The call upon the third pastor, Rev. Isaac Labagh, was approved November 19th, 1811, and he was dismissed June 15th, 1813. This was the fourth of his seven pastoral charges, and, like that of Mr. Zabriskie, his ministry extended through forty-nine years. He was licensed in 1788, and his pastoral calendar is as follows: Kinderhook, 1789–1801; Canajoharie, Stone Arabia and Sharon, 1801–1803; New Rhinebeck and Sharon, 1803–11; Greenbush and Wynantskill, 1811–14; German Church, New York city, 1815–22; New Rhinebeck, again, 1823–7; Missionary to Utica, 1827–37, when he died.

No further biographical account of this minister of Christ is accessible. He served his first church twelve years, and his last, Utica, ten; and his average in all his pastorates was seven years, yet the accessions to the church membership here were largely in excess of his predecessor, and at the close of his term, Wynantskill felt strong enough to support a pastor alone, and its connection with Greenbush was dissolved. His residence also appears to have been at Blooming Grove.

Soon after the commencement of his ministry

ISAAC LABAGH.
AT THE AGE OF 55.
(*From Oil Painting.*)

here, the Consistory resolved to discourage baptisms at private houses and strongly advised that they should be administered in the church.

Like Paul, that "Hebrew of the Hebrews," Mr. Labagh was a Dutchman of Dutchmen. His name was pronounced broadly *Labaache*, and I suspect that the prime cause of his early removal was the action of Consistory in 1812, that the English language *alone* should be used in the exercises of worship. For several years only one-third of the service had been allowed to the tongue of Mother Holland, and it was probably asking too much of a descendant of the Conferentie that he should think and write, and preach and pray only in a language foreign to his birth. The suspicion finds cogency in two facts—the pastor was absent from the Consistory meeting of December 5th, 1812, when English alone was resolved on; and secondly, he went from here to a Holland church in New York city, where he preached in Dutch only for seven years, and no doubt rejoiced at his riddance of the degenerate Reformed Dutch of Greenbush.

A notable resolution was taken in Consistory, December 25th, 1811—a Christmas greeting to the pastor:

"On motion Resolved, that whereas the call made by this Consistory on the Rev'd. Isaac Labagh, their present minister, they have agreed to allow him yearly the sum of Two hundred and sixty-five dollars, together with the use and occupation of the one-half of the parsonage and glebe; and whereas, as no free Sabbaths have been allowed the said Isaac Labagh, therefore Resolved unanimously, that until the Consistory of this church do augment the salary of Mr. Labagh to the sum of $300 annually, he be allowed yearly, and every year, two free Sabbaths."

His pastorate in this church closed seventy-three years ago, but several members of the congregation remember his ministry.

NOTE.—Mr. Labagh was instrumental in getting his younger brother, Peter, to study for the ministry. Peter afterwards became a very influential minister in the Reformed Church.—(P. T. P.)

IV.

NICHOLAS J. MARSELUS.

1815-1822.

In the year 1814 the connection of this church with Wynantskill was dissolved, and a union effected with the newly-organized church of Blooming Grove. The two congregations united in a call on Rev. Nicholas J. Marselus. The call was approved by Classis August 7th, 1815; he was ordained and installed over the two churches in

NICHOLAS J. MARSELUS.
IN HIS 79TH YEAR.

September, and dismissed March 26th, 1822. He was born in Mohawk Valley in 1792, graduated at Union College in 1810, and New Brunswick Seminary in 1815. From here he went to New York city (Greenwich) 1822–1858. After forty-three years of labor, he retired from the pastoral ministry at the age of sixty-six, and died in 1876, at the age of eighty-four. In 1844 Rutgers College gave him the degree of Doctor of Divinity.

His residence while here was at Blooming Grove. The division line between the two congregations at this time was defined as follows: "Commencing at the Rensselaer and Columbia Turnpike Road, where the road along the north side of the Cantonment intersects the first turnpike, then running eastward along the said road till near the house of Stephen Hansen, leaving Thomas I. Witbeck in Blooming Grove; then from near the said house of Stephen Hansen an easterly course, so as to leave Stephen Miller in the congregation of Greenbush."

His ministry of over six and a half years was very marked and memorable. About one hundred and fifty persons were received into membership—nearly all by confession of faith. In the year 1820 the first great revival known in Greenbush occurred, and the traditions of it are familiar to us all. Some subjects of saving grace are still living as witnesses of that shower of mercy and the faithfulness of the messenger of Christ. The report to Classis in September, 1820, was that "nearly one hundred have passed from death unto life." At a "joyful Communion season held about the middle of August, with the church overflowing, many anxious listeners filled the wagons driven up close under the windows." Dr. Marselus' subsequent ministry was very successful, but thirty years afterward he wrote: "There are many scenes which I witnessed, and consolations which I enjoyed, during that season of refreshing from the presence of the Lord, which stand out prominent among those which have marked the whole course of my protracted labors in the Gospel of the Son of God. I have enjoyed similar seasons of the right hand of the Lord in my present charge, but none equal to that which was experienced in the spring and summer of 1820."

"It is quite impossible," says Dr. Corwin, "to err in estimating the personal qualities and distinctive forces which combined in the character of Dr. Marselus. He was a man of faith and of intense convictions. He had great will power, not in any wise akin to stubbornness or obstinate prejudice, but power to abide in the service of truth and righteousness. This quality he never failed to exhibit all through his much labor and many trials. His solid and firm mind gave shape and purpose to his sermons. He preached to reach a mark. Ser-

BENJ. C. TAYLOR.

mons for him were tools to accomplish results. He believed in the power of God's Word. Converts were constantly added to his church, many of whom survive to attest his zeal and fidelity. Over thirty of these converts entered the ministry of grace, and thus extended the influence of the good man of God who had brought them to Christ."

At the commencement of his term of service both congregations adopted the new edition of the Psalm-book for use in public worship.

He was granted five "free Sabbaths" every two years.

V.

REV. BENJAMIN C. TAYLOR.

1822-1825.

Benjamin C. Taylor was born in Philadelphia February 24th, 1801, and died in Bergen, N. J., February 2d, 1881. His parents, William Taylor and Mary Alice Gazzam, were natives of Cambridge, England, and came to this country immediately after their marriage. Benjamin was their fourth son, and one of eleven children. He was converted during a revival at Baskingridge, N. J., in 1815.

"His parents had devoutly consecrated him to the Lord in his infancy. His mother especially, with a Hannah's maternal piety, had devoted him to the work of the ministry, and she followed up that consecration by a course of action which attested her sincerity and earnestness. She was one of a circle of ladies who met statedly to pray for their children and their pastor. She never mailed a letter to her absent boy at school until she had first laid it before her, and on bended knees supplicated God's blessing upon it."*

He graduated at Princeton and New Brunswick, and was licensed May 31st, 1822. Shortly after this he went into the northern part of the State of New York and visited vacant and destitute congregations in the Classes of Rensselaer and Washington. He soon received a call from the united churches of Greenbush and Blooming Grove, and about the same time another from the churches of Waterford and Schaghticoke, the former of which he accepted, and began his labors on the 10th of November following. He was ordained to the work of the ministry and installed as pastor of these two churches by the Classis of Rensselaer December 17th, 1822. On the 30th of September of that year he was united in marriage with Miss Anna Romeyn, daughter of the first pastor of this church. Immediately after their marriage at Hackensack, N. J., the youthful pair drove in a carriage to this, their new home—the parsonage in Schodack, one

---

* Dr. Van Cleef's Memorial Sermon.

mile south of this spot. He served these congregations for two years and eight months, when, finding the pastoral care of two hundred and ninety families too great, and the climate too severe, he returned to New Jersey, being called to the church of Acquackanonk, Classis of Paramus. During his work here a debt on the parsonage was paid and the languishing church greatly quickened. Rev. James R. Talmage, in a historical discourse, says of him: "He immediately began to develop those traits of character which afterward gained for him such an honorable place in the ministerial ranks."

He served Acquackanonk for three years, and in 1828 was called to the church in Bergen, where he remained fifty-three years—forty-two in active ministry and eleven as pastor emeritus—dying in 1881, in the eightieth year of his age and the fifty-ninth of his ministerial life. The church at Bergen celebrated the jubilee year of his residence among them by a grateful ovation, the associate pastor, Rev. C. Brett, preaching on the occasion the same sermon Mr. Taylor had preached there on taking charge of the church fifty years previously.

Time would fail me to tell of the tributes to his excellence of character and remarkable qualifications with which the literature of the church abounds, but I must ask you to listen to a tender monograph which his son, Rev. William James

Romeyn Taylor, of Newark, and who was born in your parsonage, has contributed to this centennial:

NEWARK, N. J., Nov. 10, 1887.

Rev. J. F. Yates:

DEAR BROTHER :—Being unable to attend the celebration of the centennial of the Reformed Church at East Greenbush, and regretting the necessity that deprives me of the pleasure of sharing the interesting service of the occasion, I comply with your request to contribute somewhat to the reminiscences of the past, by sending the accompanying brief memoranda of my father's ministry in that field.

It was his first pastoral charge, the church at Blooming Grove being then united with that of East Greenbush. He was fresh from the seminary at New Brunswick, full of zeal and enthusiasm and love for his work, and like many another young minister, he often went beyond his strength in his endeavors to fulfill his calling.

The united parishes covered a large extent of country, the people were widely scattered over it, and pastoral service at all seasons, and particularly in bad weather, and the long winters made serious inroads upon his health and shortened his period of labor there. But he never lost his attachments to the good people who warmly reciprocated his love, and valued his services in the pulpit and in their own homes.

There, too, was the anchorage of the old parsonage home, where he and my mother, both sainted now in the home above, began their happy and long married life.

His method of preaching, at first, was from manuscript sermons, carefully prepared and committed to memory. One Sabbath morning he said to my mother: "I have made such thorough preparation that I shall leave my sermon at home and preach without any notes." But in reading the scripture lesson a text struck him which took such hold of his mind, that he could not recall any part of his sermon, nor even the text. He called a deacon and sent him for the manuscript while the singing and the pastoral prayer were in progress, but the man returned, unable to find it. At last he rose and told the congregation what had happened, and said that he would try and say something about the new text that had so completely displaced his studied discourse.

"As the spirit gave him utterance," he poured forth the streams from the unsealed fountain of living truth into their souls. That was his first lesson in preaching extempore. His people felt its power and said it was the best sermon he had ever preached to them, and it changed the methods of his pulpit services. He made careful analyses, and never gave his congregations any slip-shod discourses. But excepting some special occasional efforts, and also a brief period in his later ministry, when he wrote out his sermons to shorten them, he adhered to the way into which he was led at the turning point in his early ministry.

In 1825, after nearly three years of active labors, he accepted a call from the Reformed Dutch Church at Acquackanonk, N. J. (now Passaic); a principal reason for the change being the necessity of a milder climate, and also having but one congregation to serve within smaller bounds.

The minutes of the Consistory and other records of the Greenbush Church, and that of Blooming Grove, as well, still attest the systematic order and precision of his attention to all church work—a habit which strengthened with his years, and ended only with his life. Every denominational interest that engaged his care was faithfully served in love, and nothing that he could do for his own flock, or for the church at large, was neglected or grudgingly done.

Of the immediate fruits of those first years of the nearly three score that he completed in the ministry, by the grace of God, the records may tell the story; but of their far-reaching results in the development of character and services, and in the shaping of his after life-work, none but the Lord whom he loved and served so long, can ever know.

[8]

Had he lived to celebrate with the church of his first love, this centennial commemoration, the fires of youth would have glowed again in his aged face, and in that heart that never grew cold until it ceased to beat, he would have overflowed with reminiscences which he loved to cherish and repeat.

Regretting that I cannot now add more to the interest of this memorable anniversary, I can only send my most cordial salutations "in the Lord" and remain,

Yours for Christ sake,
WILLIAM J. R. TAYLOR.

NOTE.—The writer of the above tribute to his father died very suddenly on November 12th, 1891, on the cars near Gunnison, Col., on his way to Salt Lake City, Utah, to make an address in behalf of the American Sabbath. His remains were brought to New Brunswick, N. J., and buried on November 18th, in Elmwood Cemetery. He was born at the "Greenbush parsonage" July 31st, 1823, and hence was in his sixty-ninth year at the time of his death. He was a very faithful, useful, honored minister.—(P. T. P.)

VI.

ABRAM HENRY DUMONT.

1826-1829.

Mr. Taylor was followed (September 24th, 1826), by Rev. A. H. Dumont, who, after a term of three years and three months, was dismissed December 22d, 1829. He went from this charge to Pottsville,

ABRAM H. DUMONT.

Pa.; was afterward general agent of the missionary society, and became pastor in 1833 of a Congregational church in Newport, Rhode Island, dying in 1865. He appears to have been a man of decided abilities, winning the esteem and love of his people. The Greenbush and Schodack Academy, long and justly a local pride, and to which this congregation contributed almost the whole amount of the cost of erection, was projected and partly built before he removed, and no doubt largely through his influence.

In October and November, 1829, the first addition to the church edifice was made. The Consistorial record of the enterprise is worthy of reproduction. On the 17th of October

"The committee appointed to receive proposals reported several, and it was resolved that Mr. Frederick Lasher's offer being the lowest by $600, be accepted.

"*Resolved*, That S. N. Herrick and Samuel R. Campbell be the committee to superintend the repairs.

"*Resolved*, That the following be the repairs:

"1. There shall be an addition of thirteen feet to the front of the whole building, containing one large door in front, two flights of stairs to the gallery, the old doors and windows closed, two doors to enter the body of the church—one opposite each side aisle—two recesses for stoves, one in each corner, the whole upper part of the new part floored.

"2. Across the space now occupied by the front doors, the steps to be extended, and seats made where the entrance to gallery is now.

"3. On the new part a cupola and belfry; cupola twenty feet above the eaves of the building.

"4. The whole building covered with a new roof, and said roof to be turned gable end to the road.

"6. New outside casings to the windows—the windows now in front to be closed and inserted in new part.

"7. A porch in front of large door and south door closed."

It was also "resolved that Mr. Lasher be authorized to put an arched window over the front door, and two windows on the north and two windows on the south side of the new part of the building, and a door in front of the middle aisle." This description presents us with our only picture of the church as it was in the beginning, and after its first enlargement.

The above record is followed by a list of one hundred and twenty-three subscribers to the fund for building, the amounts ranging from one to thirty dollars and averaging about seven. They must have been expeditious in those days, for in six weeks the house was re-opened for service, and the Lord's Supper administered.

But on the twenty-second of December, a few days after the re-opening, the church was surprised by the pastor's resignation. The minute is this: "Rev. A Henry Dumont presented in writing a request to be dismissed from these congregations with his reasons therefor. These being entirely satisfactory, it was resolved that, though the separation from our pastor is unexpected and painful, yet satisfied with his reasons, therefore his request be granted."

At the beginning of Mr. Dumont's ministry in 1826 the Consistories of both congregations supplied the pastor's pew with cushions. His wife, Julia Ann McKnight, was baptised and received into the church upon confession of faith. No names of persons received by him remain on the church records, all having died or moved away, but there are several who remember him. At the close of his short period of service, Blooming Grove felt herself able to support a minister alone, and in 1830 the connection was dissolved and the parsonage property divided.

NOTE.—Rev. Abram Henry Dumont, son of Peter Dumont and Elizabeth Swartout, was born at New York April 17th, 1800; licensed by Classis of New Brunswick April 20th, 1826; license signed by President John L. Zabriskie. He was called September 21st, 1826, to take charge of the churches (Dutch Reformed) of Greenbush and Blooming Grove, near Albany, N. Y. He was ordained October 17th, 1826 (but I do not know where or by whom). From Greenbush he went to Pottsville, which he left March 2d, 1831, as they could not support a Presbyterian church, so he must then have belonged to some Presbytery. He went to Newport in 1833, and preached his last sermon there in December, 1840. He was called to the First Presbyterian Church, Morristown, N. J., and preached his first sermon as pastor of that church in January, 1841, and left there in the fall of 1845. He died January 3d, 1865, and at that time belonged to some Presbytery in Connecticut. He was twice married.—(Miss E. S. Dumont, Newport, Rhode Island).

As we descend in this list of worthy names, many hearts will grow warm with the motions of deep and grateful memories.

VII.

REV. JOHN AUGUSTUS LIDDELL.
1830-1834.

On September 14th, 1830, a call was issued to Rev. John A. Liddell to serve the church of Greenbush at a salary of $400. For forty-three years

JOHN A. LIDDELL.
From a Daguerreotype.

other congregations had been associated with this, but from that time this church has supported a minister and enjoyed regular Sabbath services.

The call was accepted and he was ordained and installed on the fourteenth of November, 1830. He was dismissed on the twenty-sixth of May, 1834, after three years and six months of a memorable and blessed ministry.

Mr. Liddell was born in Scotland in 1806, educated in the University of Glasgow and in the United College of St. Andrews, and came to America about the year 1828. From this church he went to Paterson, New Jersey, for four years, thence to Lodi, New York, for the next ten, and supplied Cicero, Stone House Plains and Franklin, near Newark, N. J., the following two years. He died October 18th, 1850, at Stone House Plains, in the forty-fourth year of his age—the youngest of your translated ministers.

Mr. Liddell was a child of pious parents and of many prayers, and he passed into the kingdom he knew not when. Brethren who knew him well, write of him that he had qualities as a preacher which invested his pulpit utterances with more than ordinary power. His sermons were clear, evangelical, pungent, forcible and simple. He lacked the attraction of an attractive exterior and a graceful action, yet no one could fail to be convinced that an earnest heart prompted his solemn accents. He was a "son of consolation," wise to win souls, and possessed the faculty of attaching to himself the people of his charge in a peculiar degree. The lambs of the flock were the special objects of his attention, it is said, and that must be the reason why so many of us, who were little children when he was here, love the sound of his name and think we remember him. It was clear to all that his controlling motive was love for Christ and the souls of men. His appeals to the conscience were direct and faithful, awakening and impressive. There was a fervor and pathos in his manner that touched and melted hearts. His was the glowing ardor of one who stood between the living and the dead, and preached in view of the judgment. In life and death he bore ample testimony to the sustaining and controlling truths he preached. They say that his weakness—the one spot on this beautiful sun—was an over-sensitiveness. He shrunk from conflict and preferred to retire, when he should have stood his ground.

The second addition to the church building, some sixteen feet on the rear, was made in the year 1833.

The report of this church in 1832 speaks of a powerful revival, sixty-five persons having at that time made profession of faith; sixty-seven more were soon afterward added to the number. It was the divine seal of approval upon the people's zeal and devotion. The whole church seemed to share in the pastor's spirit. In April, 1831, the semi-annual sacrament of the Lord's Supper had been increased to quarterly, and twice in that year—January and August—Consistory had asked the congregation to set apart fifteen minutes each day, between the hours of eight and nine in the evening, for "special prayer for a blessing of divine grace to rest upon this congregation;" and the "third Tuesday in September" was observed as a day of "fasting, humiliation and prayer." The parsonage, too, adjacent to the church, was builded that year. With the offering of their hearts the people of God had given their money to His cause, and no wonder that the witnessing skies opened wide for a rain of light and love. Some few yet linger among us who were rescued from sin in that precious day of mercy, to whom this man of God was an apostle indeed, and who can say in a better than the Corinthian sense, "I am of Paul—John A. Liddell led me to Christ!"

Revival services appear to have been held during much of this year. The house was thronged, and great numbers who were at times unable to enter, gathered about the high windows in wagons, in their eagerness to see and hear. Farm work was urgent, but the people went to church. The lanes were sometimes almost impassable in the opening spring, but the thoroughly awakened people disregarded them and went. It was so at your house and it was so at ours. A relative of our family says that in that great revival our father, not then a christian, used to get up the wagon every day, and though the mud was half as deep as the wheels, take us to church. Our mother, in those days of enforced economy, left her rising bread and went to church! In the loving faith of her mother-heart she trusted that we might learn to feed on hidden manna—the Bread "of which if a man eat, he shall live forever." If my heart would suffer me, I would draw aside a sacred household curtain for the honor of our mother and our God. During that memorable revival of 1832 she gathered her children about her—probably in that evening hour which had been set apart for prayer, and as we knelt with her she prayed. Never can we forget the awe that came upon us. She talked to some One out of our sight about herself and her husband and her children. In that twilight hour we felt another Presence, and knew that her heart was burdened. We know now that she was wrestling for us—travailing in pain for her children's second birth. Blessed mother! Blessed Christ! "One generation shall praise thy works to another."

When Mr. Liddell felt it to be his duty to ask to

be dismissed, the Consistory tenderly bade him farewell and Godspeed, and passed the resolution which has been quoted again and again, and which, though quaintly and inelegantly expressed, is fit to be the watchword of any church: "*Resolved,* That we unanimously unite with each other that no division be found among us!"

"*Eendracht maakt macht.*"

NOTE.—Among some papers recently found in the possession of Mr. Liddell's only living son, I secured the following data: After coming to America he spent two years in the Theological Seminary at New Brunswick, N. J., graduating from that institution April 15th, 1830. On the fifteenth of June, the same year, he was *licensed* to preach by the Classis of New York. From his naturalization papers, we discover that he did not become a citizen of the United States of America until July 12th, 1841, when he received his papers from the *Marine Court of the City of New York.* Signed John Barberie, Clerk.

MADE CHAPLAIN.

THE PEOPLE OF THE STATE OF NEW YORK,
To All to Whom These Presents Shall Come:

KNOW YE, That pursuant to the Constitution and Laws of our said State, WE have appointed and constituted, and by these Presents do appoint and constitute John A. Liddell Chaplain of the 128th Regiment of Infantry of our said State (with rank from 30th of August, 1845), to hold the said office in the manner specified in and by our said Constitution and Laws.

IN TESTIMONY WHEREOF, We have caused our Seal for Military Commissions to be hereunto affixed. Witness, SILAS WRIGHT, Esquire, Governor of our said State, General and Commander-in-Chief of all the Militia, and Admiral of the Navy of the same, at our City of Albany, the 25th day of October in the year of our Lord one thousand eight hundred and forty-five.

SILAS WRIGHT.

Passed the Adjutant-General's Office.
THOMAS FARRINGTON, *Adjutant-General.*

Mr. Liddell's body lies buried at Totowa (Paterson), N. J. The fatal sickness was dysentery, and the duration of it only ten days. Mrs. Liddell died April 8th, 1872, aged sixty-six years and eight months. She was buried beside her husband. —(P. T. P.)

VIII.

REV. EDWARD P. STIMSON.

1834–1852.

There is less occasion as this record enters the latter half of the century that the historian should dwell upon men and their work among you, with which so many of you are familiar.

The call of the eighth pastor, Rev. Edward P. Stimson, was approved by Classis October 28th, 1834, and he was ordained and installed the following month, and dismissed in April, 1852. The semi-

E. P. STIMSON.

centennial year of the church was the third of his ministry, but no commemorative services were held. His pastorate was the longest in the history of the church, and nearly twice the average duration. During his term—in April, 1836—the bell for the tower was purchased at a cost of $337.10. It was rung twice each day for the first six months, and once a day for the next five months, partly, I believe, to accommodate the school at the Academy, and partly, no doubt, on account of its novelty.

According to the Consistory's reports to Classis, ten families were added, during his ministry, to the congregation, and the number of communicants was increased from two hundred and thirty to three hundred and fifty-five, an average of seven additions per year.

Mr. Talmage, in his published address at the laying of the corner-stone of the new church edifice on the fifth of June, 1860, says: "Rev. Edward P. Stimson, the eighth pastor, left to take charge of a new enterprise at Castleton. During his long pastorate of seventeen and a half years—some of them joyful, some sorrowful years—the following improvements may be mentioned, viz.: the addition of the north wing to the parsonage, widening of the pulpit and pews, erecting the Consistory room, hearse-house and horse-sheds, providing the church bell and procuring the musical instrument to aid in your songs of praise. The whole was so managed as to leave the church without any burden of debt —affording pleasing evidence that this congregation is willing, as well as able, when properly approached, to furnish the requisite supplies for any needed improvement.

NOTES.—On September 10th, 1841, the ladies were given permission to alter the pulpit as they saw fit.

Subscriptions amounting to $43.00 were secured October 3d, 1843, to build the hearse-house.

The horse-shed, between the church and the school house, was built in 1845, by Joseph Brockway, at a cost of $200.

On October 14th, 1848, a Mr. Witt, agent of the Western Railroad Co., gave the Consistory $148.50.

On December 22d, 1852, thirteen persons received certificates from this church to unite with the newly-organized Reformed Church at Castleton, of which Mr. Stimson became the first pastor.

He is remembered by the people of East Greenbush as a man of splendid physique, of very unusual executive abilities, and as having decided gifts as a preacher. He continued to exercise the office of a minister until 1861, after which he lived in quiet retirement at Castleton, and died there in 1876, in the seventy-first year of his age. His body rests in the cemetery at Castleton.—(P. T. P.)

JAMES R. TALMAGE.

IX.

REV. JAMES R. TALMAGE.
1852–1860.

Rev. Mr. Talmage commenced his labors October 1st, 1852, and concluded them February 1st, 1860, serving a little over seven years.

His ministry reached the period of seven years and four months. He was licensed in 1829, and preached successively at Pottsville, Pa., Jersey City, Pompton Plains, Blawenburgh, Athens, Brooklyn, Greenbush, Chittenango, Warwarsing and Wiltwick. He "ceased at once to work and live," and left behind him multitudes to thank God that they ever knew him, and to mourn his departure. His widow, whom also you loved and revered, survives.

Accepting a call to Chittenango, Mr. Talmage kindly consented to give his influence to the project for a new church edifice, and in a few days procured $5,000 in subscriptions, assuring success, and in the same year this second "house of prayer" was erected, at a cost, some say, of $8,000. The first reports to Classis of the "Religious and Benevolent contributions" of this church were made by Mr. Talmage, beginning with the year 1854.

Rev. Dr. Goyn Talmage, his brother, sends us the following affectionate tribute to his memory:

Port Jervis, N. Y., Nov. 15, 1887.

Rev. J. F. Yates:

Dear Brother:—You have requested me, either personally or by letter, to represent my brother, Rev. James R. Talmage, at the one hundredth anniversary of the East Greenbush Reformed Church. As I am providentially prevented from participating in the very interesting services of the occasion, I will avail myself of the opportunity of writing a few words of him who served in the pastorate of that church from 1852 to 1860.

Were I to attempt a full portrayal of the excellent qualities and life of James R. Talmage, the article would be regarded an exaggeration, except by those who were intimately associated with him as personal friends, or as his parishioners. All who were brought in close contact with him in the different Classes to which he belonged, and the congregations he served, will heartily endorse what I am about to write.

Dr. James R. Talmage was singularly pure in his life and conversation. He kept his heart so carefully that it was manifest his conduct was shaped and his words spoken as under the Divine eye, and with a view to the Divine approval. While he was a cheerful companion, and enjoyed and contributed to the enjoyment of social life, yet he never forgot for a moment, or failed to impress others, that he was a christian.

As a preacher of the Gospel he held forth the word of truth with more than ordinary ability and with peculiar painstaking. Maintaining all through his ministry the study of the Scriptures in their original languages, he endeavored to give the mind of the Spirit in those portions which he brought to the pulpit for exposition. His sermons were rich in doctrine and highly practical. They were prepared with exceeding care, with dependence upon the Holy Spirit for guidance. He seldom left a text until he brought out about all there was in it. Nothing worried him so much as to be compelled from force of circumstances to bring unbeaten oil to the service of the sanctuary. His hearers could not but acknowledge that they had opportunity of being built up in the things of the Kingdom. His pastoral work out of the pulpit was faithfully and prayerfully performed. He felt the burden of souls upon him, and for more than fifty years ceased not publicly and from house to house to teach and preach Jesus Christ.

Possessed of an exceedingly humble and modest spirit, he was absolutely without ambition for prominence, and even shrunk from positions to which his brethren thought he was entitled, and where his usefulness would be greatly enlarged. By reason of the meekness of his spirit, his real worth and force of character were but little known beyond the immediate neighborhoods where his ministry was exercised; but his spiritual mindedness, and christian example, and patient toil for souls, rendered his work faithful in every place where his Master sent him. The impression he made on his people was, that he was Christlike in temper and life, and therefore a pattern to be followed. He was extremely careful of the reputation of his ministerial brethren, and being himself devoid of envy, always rejoiced in their promotion to honor and usefulness. He manifested less resentment than any man with whom I have had association, with a single exception. When suffering wrongfully he never upbraided, but sought to excuse the wrong-doer by pointing out the palliating circumstances with which the mistake had originated.

He had three brothers (all yet living), who at various periods followed him in the holy office, to all of whom he was exceedingly helpful. They all recognize their deep indebtedness to him, and thank God to-day that in their early ministry they had before them such a striking example of pastoral devotion and faithfulness, and do not hesitate to acknowledge that any measure of success they may have attained, they owe in no small degree, under God, to their elder brother, now gone to his eternal reward.

A whole generation has passed away since James Talmage came to minister to the congregation at East Greenbush, but there are doubtless not a few of the fathers and mothers still remaining there who talk of him to their children and hold his life among them in fresh and precious and grateful remembrance.

May this review of the history of your church, calling up afresh the faithfulness of God to its pastors and people for one hundred years, be fruitful in rich spiritual blessings to all whose privilege it shall be to join in the jubilee.

Faithfully yours,
GOYN TALMAGE.

NOTE.—The three brothers referred to in the above letter were (1) Rev. John V. N. Talmage, D.D., who has spent the most of his life since 1847 in the mission field at Amoy, China, but is now living at Bound Brook, N. J., in feeble health; (2) Rev. Goyn Talmage, D.D., the writer of the letter, who died suddenly at Somerville, N. J., June 24th, 1891, in the seventieth year of his age; and (3) Rev. T. DeWitt Talmage, D.D., of Brooklyn, N. Y., whose name and fame are world-wide.

Items of Record.—On February 1st, 1853, the Classis tried to settle the boundary line between Castleton and East Greenbush congregations by suggesting that it be a straight line running from the north part of the farm of Joachim Staats, on the Hudson river, to the farm of Mr. Warden, on the turnpike. This was opposed by Rev. Mr. Talmage as improper and unjust. The final agreement is not recorded.

In 1855 two acres of land were purchased from

Walter Morrison for a burying ground. The price paid was $400, and enough to cancel the ground rent. The next year a fence was built around it at a cost of $100.

A resolution was passed by Consistory September 2d, 1859, that funds be raised to clear the brambles from the burial ground.

In the winter of 1859 and '60 the question of building a new church was earnestly agitated. On January 6th, 1860, David Rector was appointed to ascertain the prospects of purchasing the Academy grounds.

On January 10th a congregational meeting was held to consider the proposition of building a church. Of this meeting the Rev. James R. Talmage said, at the laying of the corner-stone on June 5th, 1860: "Who of us can forget that memorable Tuesday in January last, when, assembled in the old church, after a spirited discussion, in which invited friends kindly and mightily assisted us, it was resolved that we must have a new church, and that as soon as five thousand dollars were secured, the building committee should proceed? And who that was present on the following Sabbath can forget the joyfulness of the people, when the chairman of the subscription committee announced from the desk that the required amount was secured? The good work has been going on steadily. I have not been present to witness the steps, but sure I am that it has been going on; there are convincing proofs—huge piles of weighty arguments all around us. May God continue to smile upon the enterprise, bringing it to a successful issue. He will—He will, only mind, looking to the hills whence help cometh, to lift each one according to his ability, lifting together, and continuing to lift with good courage, and every muscle streethed, until the topmost stone is laid. Amen."

On the sixteenth of January, 1860, the following building committee was appointed: Henry Salisbury, David Rector, John Van Denbergh, Jacob Kimmey, Henry Lodewick, and discretionary power was given then to buy a new lot to build the church upon, near the old site. After much consultation, it was determined to build on the old site.

At first it was resolved to build of *wood*, but eventually, on April 7th, 1860, the architect's plan was approved and they resolved to build of *brick*. During that season the building operations were hurried along with all possible speed, under the direction of Mr. A. Birch, master builder. By the next spring the new church was ready for dedication, and on April 3d, 1861, the Consistory decided to hold those exercises on the twenty-fourth day of the present month.—(P. T. P.)

REV. J. R. TALMAGE'S LETTER AT DEDICATION.

CHITTENANGO, April 15, 1861.

To the Church and Congregation of East Greenbush:

BRETHREN AND FRIENDS:—I have never lost sight of the promise I made, more than a year ago, that I would endeavor to be with you at the time of the dedication of your new church; but in the orderings of Providence you have fixed the time when necessary engagements connected with the regular meeting of our Classis will prevent my attendance. The best, therefore, I can do is to be present in spirit.

I fancy I see the new church in its attractive comeliness, and a large congregation of well-remembered faces assembled to unite in the solemn yet joyful dedicatory exercises. "Lord, it is good for us to be here," in circumstances so cheering as well as impressive. What a change has come over our place of worship! Behold the transfiguration! None who were present will soon forget the stirring meeting held on this spot on Tuesday, January 8th, of last year, when, after conference, it was voted so unanimously and earnestly, beyond all expectation, that the church edifice here was unattractive, uncomfortable and not altogether safe. If our eyes and feelings decided correctly, then verily there has occurred a marvelous transformation. Behold, now, how attractive as well as comfortable and safe, so far as man is capable of seeing and knowing. What meaneth this? The Lord stirred up the heart of the subscription committee to go forward with flaming zeal, and the hearts of the people to subscribe with courageous liberality, so that on the ensuing Sabbath the pulpit gladly announced that $5,000 had been subscribed. Then the Lord stirred up the building committee with painstaking zeal and tireless perseverance, in their work so responsible and difficult. Then the Lord stirred up the builder, as He does every wise master builder, to lay the foundations deep and broad.

On the fifth day of June last, a joyful assembly—the sky favoring—witnessed the laying of the corner-stone with appropriate ceremonies, since which time the busy workmen, with muscular arms, have been plying their tools and lifting higher and higher, until behold, the topmost stone is laid, and we shout, "grace, grace unto it." Let every one who has labored faithfully in whatever department of this good work have due praise, and let the chief praise be given to Him, without whose gracious promptings and aid not a copper would have been given, or a finger lifted. All the way, step by step, His favoring providence has led, working in us both to will and to do.

It is good to be here in this new temple, on this hallowed spot. Stirring reminiscences of the past come thronging up and mingling with the joyful solemnities of the occasion. Here, in a former edifice, three times three successive pastors have preached and prayed, breaking to hungry souls the bread of life. The first three, viz., Romeyn, Zabriskie and Labagh, spent the alternate Sabbaths at Wynantskill, excepting during the first few years, when Mr. Romeyn officiated alternately at Schodack. These three, each, after a pilgrimage of more than three score years and ten, went to their reward, and scarce an individual is left of all those brought into the communion of this church during their ministry.

The next three successive pastors, viz., Marselus, Taylor and Dumont, spent the alternate Sabbaths with the new church at Blooming Grove. These still live to proclaim the glorious Gospel. During the last year of Mr. Dumont's labors here (1829), the congregation gave liberally for the complete remodeling of the church edifice, thus enriching themselves, through God's blessing, so much, that ever since they have been fully able to support the ministry.

The first one of the remaining three pastors whose undivided labors have been given here, viz., J. A. Liddell, after laboring very successfully, here and elsewhere, while yet in the prime of life, was called home. Who knows but tidings may have already reached him, and the other deceased pastors, through some swift-winged messenger, enabling them to share in the joy of this occasion, so interesting in the history of a church for whose welfare they toiled and prayed on earth.

The next pastor, E. P. Stimson, labors in an adjoining field, and the last, J. R. Talmage, desires, in the best way he can, to contribute his mite towards promoting the interest of the occasion. This has been a heaven-favored church. She has, indeed, had her times of trial. What church has not? She has been specially tried by the calling away of her pastors to other fields of labor, generally before they had reached their prime. But the great Shepherd always had some one in process of preparation, just ready to step in and occupy the vacancy, so that she has never been long in a state of widowhood. The last vacancy has been the longest. We found it hard, mutually, to part, but how happy has been the result. God, in that hour of trial, helped us to work together, starting the church building enterprise, the result of which surpasses our expectations. By the same event the Lord stirred up the people of my present charge to the good work of building an excellent parsonage. He has also, meanwhile, furnished you with stated preaching, during most of the time, on every alternate Sabbath, by one ripe in christian and pastoral experience. This providential supply relieved you from the necessity of exposing your pastor to the interruptions, distractions, collisions, financial contrivings and various perils connected with church building, which are so apt to spill on the ground a pastor's influence. To-day you are in more favorable circumstances than ever you were before to gain the ear of a suitable minister, several times more favorable than when you sat trembling with cold or fear in the old building. Your recent liberality in building a house for Him, the Lord will reward, in answers to your prayers, with a workman that needeth not to be ashamed, and with spiritual blessings through his ministry, such as were not received and not to be expected, so long as the Lord's house was lying waste in the midst of a people dwelling in their ceiled houses.

"It is good to be here." Hallowed reminiscences of the past, including times of gracious refreshing from on high, and present associations and exercises well adapted to move and cheer the soul, together with bright anticipations for the future, combine to emphasize the declaration—meet here, my friends, oft as you can, to get all the good you can, and you'll find it good to be here beyond what I can tell or you can conceive—good for soul and body—for time and eternity—good for all within the sweep of your good influence. He is faithful that promised.

The Lord send thee help from the sanctuary and strengthen thee out of Zion; remember all thy offerings, and accept thy burnt sacrifice. Selah. Affectionately yours, &c.,

J. R. TALMAGE.

OBITUARY NOTICE BY REV. DR. VAN SANTVOORD, OF KINGSTON, N. Y.

The death of this devoted and beloved minister took place on Sabbath evening, June 29th, 1879, in the seventy-second year of his age, and just after completing fifty years of ministerial labor. He died at the house of his son-in-law, Rev. James Wyckoff, pastor of the Reformed Church of Germantown, N. Y. He had gone there for a fortnight's rest, to recruit from the effects of what his family and friends considered but a slight attack of illness. They hoped to see him return after this interval, strengthened to resume his work. It was ordered otherwise by Him who orders all things well. The disease which seemed little serious at first, assumed after several days a sterner form,

PETER Q. WILSON.

settling at last into fever, which held him with unrelaxing grip many days. When consciousness returned at last, the bodily forces were too far gone to be rallied and he passed tranquilly away into "the city which hath foundations," towards which it had been his heart's joy during all his long and fruitful ministry to direct the steps of way-worn, sin-laden pilgrims, and for entering which he stood ever ready "with loins girded about and lights burning when the summons should reach him to join the company of the redeemed." He was interred in the Wiltwick Cemetery at Kingston, N. Y.

X.

REV. PETER Q. WILSON.

1861-1866.

The tenth pastor, Rev. Peter Quick Wilson, was born at Roycefield, New Jersey, graduated at Rutgers College in 1858 and New Brunswick Seminary in 1861. Accepting a call to this church in that year, he was ordained and installed as pastor on the eighth day of October, Revs. Benjamin F. Snyder, J. B. Wilson, J. R. Talmage and Elbert Nevius officiating. He was the first minister in the new church edifice, and served as pastor between four and five years, leaving here June 1st,

1866. From here he went to Spencertown and took charge of the Presbyterian Church. He has also served the churches of Guttenburg, Ponds and Rockland, where he now has charge of a Presbyterian church. Mr. Wilson and Dr. John Steele are the only surviving ministers of the twelve. It is matter for congratulation that not only is he spared to proclaim the Gospel he loves, but cheers us by his presence to-day. It is but just that the historian should say that the standard of pulpit ministrations to which you had been accustomed, was amply maintained by Mr. Wilson. A church debt of nearly $3,000 was paid, and a new *iron fence* for the front and the west side of the church, costing $400, was built and paid for. The income from the pews of the new church was sufficient for the pastor's, sexton's and chorister's salaries, and to provide fuel and light.

To the reports of benevolent collections to Classis, begun by Mr. Talmage in 1854, Mr. Wilson added annual reports of moneys raised by this church for "congregational purposes." For the first sixty-six years no such reports were made, and no documents have been found showing the "benevolent" contributions of the church during that period. But since 1854 there have been thirty reports of such collections, aggregating $6,915.23; and since 1861, when Mr. Wilson began to report contributions for "congregational purposes," there have been twenty-four reports, aggregating $63,609.23.

NOTES.—Newspaper item published some time in 1866, giving a brief account of the work accomplished under Mr. Wilson's ministry and of the esteem in which he was held by the people:

"NO MORE DEBT.—The congregation of the Reformed Protestant Dutch Church of East Greenbush paid their last item of debt during the month of April. The church edifice is new. They commenced the work of building in 1860. In April, 1861, the church was dedicated to the worship and service of Almighty God. In the ensuing October they selected a pastor, P. Q. Wilson, a licentiate from our Theological Seminary. At that time the debt was not quite $3,000. This debt has been paid, and we rejoice and are glad. The fence was old. Times hard. War and taxes caused many complaints. The pastor and children gave a few concerts, raised the money, and erected a neat iron fence, at a cost of $400. This was the children's offering. Steps have been provided; and last, but not least, a new organ, which we hope will prove a satisfaction to all. The church is large and substantial. Great care has been taken in furnishing the house. In fact, it is very seldom that you find a church in the country whose internal arrangements and finish give so many marked expressions of culture and intelligence. It is an honor to all who have thus exhibited their love for Christ in building a house for His glory. The struggle has been great, but the results of the six years fill our hearts with praise and thanksgiving to the Lord who has owned our work and prospered Zion.

"And it is our delightful privilege to record the prosperity of church and Sabbath-school as the brightest chapter in the history of this Zion. Our pastor, whose voice has been somewhat weakened by a recent attack of diphtheria, resigned the charge of this important field the *first Sabbath in May*. His labors have received the highest approbation of our people, and given evidence of God's favor resting upon them. And when he was ready to close this faithful ministry, the people manifested their kindness and benevolence in a very touching manner, viz., a present of $200, and from a few choice friends, a valuable gold watch. And we are happy to say that these gifts are illustrative of that blessed spirit of christian kindness which has characterized his ministry.   TRUTH."

The Organ.—On February 6th, 1866, the Consistory entered into an agreement with George N. Andrews, of Utica, N. Y., to furnish an organ of the best materials and workmanship, to be delivered in ten weeks and to be kept in repair for ten

WILLIAM ANDERSON.

years, at a cost of $1,050. This contract was fulfilled, and for twenty-five years this instrument has led a devout people in their praises to Almighty God.

Mr. Wilson is the only pastor now living of the twelve who served the church during the first century. His parish is at Fawns, N. Y., near Saugerties, where he labors with true apostolic zeal, receiving at least the approval of St. Paul, who said, "He that is unmarried is careful for the things of the Lord, how he may please the Lord."
—(P. T. P.)

XI.

REV. WILLIAM ANDERSON.

1866–1876.

The ministerial death-knell has struck in this centennial year, and the spirit of your eleventh pulpit teacher has entered into final rest. Rev. William Anderson took charge of this church—the fourth and last but one in his history—in 1866, and retired in 1876. His pastorate here was a very noticeable and active one. The Academy, which had been closed for some time, was re-opened through his instrumentality and flourished for several years. In 1872 the new and spacious parsonage was erected, and the interests of the church generally seem to have been promoted. His affection for his people was a striking characteristic, and he cherished them as fathers, brothers, children. His previous fields of labor were Peapack, N. J., Fairview, Ill., and Newtown, N. Y., and the subsequent one, and in which he died last April, Fordham, New York City. He gave a son to the ministry, who takes his father's place here to-day, and whose noblest ambition and fittest prayer might be to honor that father's name in this holy calling, and conquer at last like him.

A few days previous to his death, Miss Fanny Van Vechten, of Castleton, visited him. He realized that his strength was failing, and expressing the belief that he should never again look upon your faces on earth, sent by her his dying message to the church. Miss Van Vechten says:

"I was at Mr. Anderson's in April, and left there only a week before he died, and while knowing he was very miserable, still we did not dream the end was so near, though I think, perhaps, he himself felt he was drawing near to the 'golden gates.'

"One morning, as I was alone with him, he said: 'Fanny, I fear I shall never see East Greenbush again, but I want you to take a message for me to that people; tell them I loved them as I never loved any other people with whom I have been connected, that I have remembered them at the throne of grace, and that I ask them so to live that, if I never see them again on earth, I may greet each one in our heavenly home, not a single one be missing. Tell them to love their pastor, love their church and work for it, giving their best strength, their means, and supporting and upholding it as their highest earthly good and pleasure; but, above all, and before all, give their whole hearts to their Saviour, and in God's own good time, I will meet them again in a better, even a heavenly home.' These are as nearly Mr. Anderson's own words as I can recall them, and in doing so I seem to see again his face and patient suffering, its meekness, but above all, its sweetness and love as he spoke of this people."

NOTES.—It is but just to the memory of Mr. Anderson that a few items be added to the foregoing history. He acted such a conspicuous part in a general uplifting of the congregation, that his ten years of service might with propriety be called a transitional period. His labors began November 1st, 1866, and ceased October 15th, 1876.

The purchase of the Staats' lot furnished the first opportunity for the display of his executive ability in the management of the temporal affairs of the congregation. With keen foresight he saw a suitable site on this plot for new horse-sheds, and early in 1867 had the project well under way. That year thirty-two stalls were built, Henry Salisbury doing the carpenter work. A little later, perhaps the next year, four more were built, connecting the western ends of the two long rows. Since that time seven more have been added to the eastern end of one row and four more to that of the other row, making a total of forty-seven stalls. What a convenience and comfort these are, those only can appreciate who have to drive miles to attend a house of worship. Here beast and vehicle are always protected from heat and cold and storm, and in a country parish this does a great deal to solve the problem of regular attendance upon divine service.

Again, with equal sagacity, he urged the choice of the middle lot for a new parsonage. When this undertaking was completed, about the middle of his pastorate, every one could see how wise the choice had been. Mr. Anderson was especially interested in the improvement of the educational and social conditions of the community. First by a private school in the old parsonage, under the care of one daughter, and later in the large school in the academy, under the management of his three daughters and two assistants, he was instrumental in changing the tastes and aspirations of scores of young men and maidens who might otherwise have continued in the "good old way" of the district school, and settled down to a hum-drum life. His large and interesting family co-operated to the fullest extent in all his plans and desires for the welfare of the people. Their sacrifices and labors have left an impression that time cannot efface. They did much to elevate the tone of society and to purify the morals of the community. The congregation's appreciation of all those factors of strength was shown before the end of the first year of his ministry by a very decided increase of support.

On October 9th, 1867, the Consistory raised the salary from $900 per year to $1,300. In addition to this a number of liberal donations augmented the comfort and joy of the pastor's household from time to time. Early the next spring the assessment on the pews was increased *one-half*, and this was to continue " during the present pastorate."

In the year 1868 the exterior of the church was painted for the first time. The work was done by Robert Ketchum at a cost of $306.00 It is commonly known that the district school house, the second story of which is the "old Consistory room," stands upon the property of the church. At different times the question of enlarging the present building or erecting a new school house has been agitated. The matter was talked of in 1869. The action of the Consistory on July 17th of that year on this question was as follows: That the district have the privilege of erecting a new school house on the same site, but increased to the size of thirty feet square and to front the road for an annual rent of thirty dollars. The proposition was not accepted, for the old house still stands. The year 1870 was eventful in trying to settle the question about a parsonage. Some thought it wise to sell the old and build a new one; others saw only difficulty and debt ahead, and advised selling the Staats property and keeping the old house. But, however, a subscription was started for a new parsonage, which very soon reached the amount of $1,500. Here it was deemed best to let the matter rest for a time. This was early in the year. About that time the church had an opportunity to sell a part of the Staats lot to the Misses Yates, and they decided to let them have three-quarters of an acre. This helped in the solution of the problem. But on October 12th, the record states, the Consistory decided to buy Mr. George Shibley's property—house, barn and about two acres of ground—adjoining the old parsonage, and then sell and dispose of the old parsonage building. Negotiations in this direction ended, however, when it was learned that Mr. Shibley wanted $4,000 for his property. During that season the flag-walks were laid in front of the church. In February, 1871, it was resolved to sell the corner lot of the new parsonage grounds. On the fifteenth of April, 1872, a committee reported subscriptions to the amount of $2,600, with more promised. This gave the required impetus to the new parsonage movement. With the choice lot reserved and this sum pledged, even though the old property had not been sold, the people saw their opportunity and proceeded to build the elegant house that now adorns the grounds. The old parsonage was sold the next winter. A complaint was made by Mr. Simeon Allen that the water from the church sheds ran upon his property to the detriment of the same. A meeting was held on February 28th, 1872, of the Consistory, shed owners and those who rented sheds to consider this allegation. It was soon after decided that action could not be instituted against the church, since each individual owned the shed he used, and suit, if any, must be brought against every such person separately. Quit-claim deeds were given to owners of sheds March 8th, 1872.

These, and many other things, like the management of the academy with twenty boarders and sixty day pupils, show how necessary it was that one with marked ability in business affairs should have been at the head of these changes and movements. But there is another side to Mr. Anderson's ministry, and that is the chief side—the spiritual. He was a careful, exegetical student of the Word. His sermons were logical, direct and well illustrated. All classes profited by his preaching, and the church at times was too limited to accommodate the audiences. He ever sought to bring to every one that truth that he felt was best calculated to awaken a new life. Revivals took place and many bless him as their "father in Christ."

The last Sabbath he officiated was October 15th, 1876. On the afternoon of that day the Lord's Supper was celebrated.

When he retired from the pastorate of this people he accepted a call to the Reformed Church of Fordham, New York City, where he lived and labored until the close of his life in April, 1887.

At a meeting of Consistory held September 25th, 1876, the resignation of Rev. William Anderson was accepted, and the following resolutions unanimously passed :

Resolved, That in sundering the cherished ties which have bound us together during the past ten years, we tender our pastor our affectionate veneration for his wise counsels and able expositions of Divine truth, and for his ardent solicitude for our temporal, and especially for our spiritual prosperity ;

Resolved, That we will ever remember with satisfaction and gratitude the precious and marked results of his labors among us in the Lord.

Resolved, That our best wishes and prayers will follow him to his new field of labor, earnestly hoping that in the good providence of God he may long continue to prosecute the Gospel ministry, and be crowned with continuous and abundant success.

GEO. B. MILLS, *Moderator*.

It was with great fortitude that Mr. Anderson carried on his work, at times maintaining a severe struggle with failing health, but always cheerful and hopeful, until at last on the twenty-third day of April, 1887, the Master said "come up higher," and his spirit took its flight to the better world to minister in the immediate presence of Him who sits upon the throne. His familiar form we laid tenderly to rest in Woodlawn Cemetery, New York City, on Tuesday, April 26th, 1887. He was in the seventy-third year of his age and in the thirty-eighth of his ministry.—(P. T. P.)

RESOLUTIONS PASSED AT EAST GREENBUSH.

The Consistory of the Reformed Church of East Greenbush, Rensselaer County, New York, has received the sad intelligence of the death of the Rev. William Anderson, their former pastor for ten years.

His eminent learning and devoted piety combined to make him conscientious and successful as a minister of Christ; his faithful labors for the conversion of the unsaved, the edification of the faithful and upbuilding of Zion, and his zeal in the cause of education, all endeared him alike to the young and the old of this community; therefore,

Resolved, That the church express their deep sorrow at his death, and offer their heartfelt sympathy to his bereaved family, commending them to the God of all comfort, and joining them in the hope and consolation of the blessed promise of a glorious immortality.

Resolved, That a copy of the foregoing minute be sent to the bereaved family and also to the *Christian Intelligencer* for publication.

By order of the Consistory.

Adopted May 4th, 1887.

XII.

REV. JOHN STEELE, D.D.

1877–1887.

> "As your guide,
> He in the heavenward path hath firmly walked,
> Bearing your joys and sorrows on his breast,
> And on his prayers. He at your household hearths
> Hath spoke His Master's message; while your babes,
> Listening, imbibed, as blossoms drink the dew;
> And when your dead were buried from your sight,
> Was he not there?"

The last survivor of Christ's apostles was John, whose antitype in the pleasant parallel I have been

JOHN STEELE.

suggesting, is the latest shepherd of this flock. Yonder, fifty leagues away, he lies resting his weary head on Jesus' bosom and counting the throbbings of the blessed Saviour's heart.

We all remember too well how sudden was the dreadful blow. In the fullness of his powers, in the midst of a very fruitful ministry with his commission ringing fresh as ever in his ears and his heart yearning for the souls of men; in the study which had so long witnessed his meek searching of the Holy Word, and his prayers for help in proclaiming it—on the evening of December 7th, 1886, that commission seemed to be annulled, and the Master to say, "It is enough."

His last service, December 5th, had been to preach the Gospel, administer the Lord's Supper, baptize Maria Boughton, and receive her into the fellowship of the church.

His parents were Nehemiah Vernon Steele and Sophia Garretson, and he was born at Somerville, Somerset county, New Jersey, September 20th, 1827. At the age of fourteen years he united with the Reformed Church in his native place. He was educated at Rutgers College and New Brunswick Seminary, and has preached in Lebanon, N. J., Union Village and Coxsackie, N. Y., and Totowa, N. J., and for the last ten years as pastor of this church. For several years he has contemplated this anniversary, and it is greatly to be deplored that he could not have written the history of this church from the standpoint of its centennial pastor. At his home in Newark last month he gave me for you his christian greetings for this day—to which for years he had looked forward in hope—and he has also sent you by his own trembling hand the letter from his heart to which you have listened.

It may or may not be that the spirits of departed friends re-visit this world in these latter days, but if ever they come back, they must be here to-day. Gathered as we are to recall their life-work and catch new impulse for our own, to praise their devotion and pray for a double portion of their spirit, it is easy to think that the gates are ajar, and the throngs all around us. No picture gallery in the world could equal for us this temple, were these walls covered with the portraits of those hundreds gone, the godly dead, whose diamond dust lies here and there and yonder in many an angel-hovered grave. But even their pictures, looking down upon us here, might grow too sacred in our reverence— worshiping the images of the saints!

[At the suggestion of the historian the congregation was asked to indicate, by rising, their recollection of the pastors of the church, beginning with the last—Dr. Steele. Almost all of the vast assembly rose. Next, those who remembered his predecessor, Mr. Anderson, were asked to remain standing and others to be seated, and so on through the list in the inverse order of their settlement. It was a spectacle never to be forgotten, as name after name was called, to see the number melting down, until Dr. Marselus was reached, when but two or three remained standing. No one present remembered to have seen Labagh, Zabriskie or Romeyn].

Time has forbidden that I should give, as I should have been glad to do, the many words of confidence and love and gratitude with which the officers of this church, from time to time, have parted with its pastors. It must have been a most welcome encouragement to the minister when resigning his trust, that his confidential advisers—the men who knew him best—so cheerfully gave him their thanks and their prayers.

Three unsuccessful calls are all I have been able to trace, though the records may be defective. Most of the removals were occasioned by "calls" to other fields, and this church in turn disturbed other congregations by similar overtures. When we stop to think of it, there is a flavor of selfishness in this invading a sister church with a bold bid to take away their chosen settled pastor for yourselves. But all the denominations do it. There is a unique scrap of history of such an instance, which is so rare a curiosity that I must not withhold it: Dr. J. C. Freyenmoet, who preached some years in Schodack and hereabout before this church was organized, and whose name (sometimes spelled Fremont) appears in many of your old family records of baptism, had when a young man been sent to Holland, as the custom then was, to be educated for the ministry. The expense of his education was borne by a single church, with the understanding that on his return he should serve the church which had sent him out. He was accordingly duly installed as pastor. But after some six months had elapsed, another sound Dutch church in the vicinity made overtures to the bright ecclesiastic to honor their call, and an increased salary, by coming over to their Macedonia. When the old congregation heard of it the blood was all up, to be sure, and they promptly met the occasion. Here is their missive, such as probably has rarely been equaled in its combination of scripture texts and human resentments, the Divine Gospel and the civil law, submission to the will of God and resistance to the church of "Rochester":

To the Consistory of Rochester, Greetings:

We, your servants, having been informed and concluded therefrom that you have had correspondence with our Preacher, and have in so far seduced him as to send him a call, and think by the amount of money to take him away from us, but that Lord who has hitherto hindered your underhand game, shall further direct it to a good result, therefore we find ourselves in duty bound, in accordance with the words of the Saviour, "Do good to those who do evil to you," etc., so will we in time to come do good to you as we have in the past, for which you do not thank us that he hath served you.

And then you dare say that he hath eight free Sundays in each year, which is as true as the words of the Devil to Eve, "Ye shall not surely die." But if you desire to have our Preacher four or six times in the year, we shall by no means refuse you, but will leave it to our Preacher to bargain as to the compensation for his services. And if this cannot prevent the execution of your unjust intention, and the Lord sees fit to use you as a rod to chasten us, we shall accept it as coming from the hand of the Lord, and comfort ourselves with the blessed saying of Paul, Hebrews 12: "For whom the Lord loveth He chasteneth, and scourgeth every son whom He receiveth." And if the Lord hath foreseen that you shall have our Preacher, then nevertheless we do not hope that your consciences will be so seared as to take away with him a part of our livelihood, being the sum of £125, 12s., 6d.,[*] otherwise we shall feel bound to leave the matter

---

[*] Money they had paid for his education.

to the Civil Court. We expect an answer to this, and conclude our reasons with "The grace of our Lord Jesus Christ, the love of God the Father, and the communion of the Holy Ghost remain with you until a blessed eternity." Amen.

We remain your servants,
   Signed.   JAN KORTRECHT,
         JAN VAN VLIEDT,
         ABRAHAM VAN CAMP,
         WILLIAM COOL.

I testify to the above in behalf of the whole Consistory. JOH. CASPARUS FREYENMUTH,
          Preaching Elder.

Done at a meeting of Consistory at Machackermech, 6th day of Dec., 1741.

There are no records of the nature of the communication of the Consistory of this church with that of Millstone, when Mr. Zabriskie was charmed away from here by their call—but if that Millstone did not feel that it was a *nether* Millstone before it came finally to the top—then the signs, protest to Classis, special Classis, etc., have little significance.

In those old days the domine was a man in society, and in the state, with a sharp eye on public affairs; and the Dutch domine, at least, a man of very positive convictions. It is stated of one in a neighboring county that in the famous times of Andrew Jackson he led a file of men to the polls to vote for "Old Hickory," and so great was his influence that only one man, out of a total of 701, voted against Jackson!

And not only in religion and in politics, but in love as well, was he straightforward and direct. Here is a model love-letter, written not many miles from here, by which domine Rynier Van Nest won his bride:

"Respected and Beloved Catharine Goetschius: My desire is to have you for my wife, if you will consent. Your friends at Schoharie have recommended you to me. If you will consent, then write me at your earliest convenience and I will come and see you. RYNIER VAN NEST."

There was no coquetry about Catharine; the frank proposal met with an equally frank acceptance, and they were married within four weeks.

NOTES.—After the retirement of Mr. Anderson the pulpit remained vacant seven months before a successor was found. On June 5th, 1877, the Consistory decided to call Rev. John Steele, D.D., of Paterson, N. J. This call was accepted, but Dr. Steele did not begin his labors until in August. His installation took place October 30th, 1877. He continued his pastoral duties with eminent ability and genial affability for a little over nine years, when suddenly, without the slightest intimation, he was stricken with paralysis. He lingered along during the winter with doubtful hope of recovery until, being convinced that he was permanently disabled, on May 1st, 1877, he offered his resignation. This was reluctantly accepted, and the congregation continued his salary to October 1st, 1887, and desired his family to remain in the parsonage. They, however, thought it best to remove to Newark, N. J., to be near their kindred. Here he passed the remnant of his days, so far rallying at times as to see his friends, to walk out some and to attend divine services and take some lesser part in the exercises. Indeed, on the Thursday evening previous to his death, he had taken part in the prayer meeting with peculiar force and earnestness. Says one: "Dr. Steele was especially favored in being surrounded by a family of great culture and refinement, who were able to, and did, sustain him in every good work, in the church, in the Sunday school, in the prayer meetings and wherever they could lend a helping influence. The most affectionate remembrances, and the warmest testimonials of love and appreciation will ever be theirs."

His death occurred suddenly at his home on January 17, 1889. Thus he lingered only a few days over two years and one month after his first stroke. He remarked to a classmate a short time before his departure: "My work is done; I am willing to go; I am only watching and waiting."

His blameless christian life, his wise counsels and his great zeal for the cause of Christ will ever keep his memory dear to this people.

He was in the sixty-second year of his age and the forty-first of his ministry. His body rests in Fairmount Cemetery, Newark, N. J.—(P. T. P.)

I must pass over chapters relating to the church edifices here and at Wynantskill and Blooming Grove; the parsonages on the turnpike and at Blooming Grove; the sale of the land leased to the church, subject to a trifling rental; the alteration of the pews from the old square form in which nearly half of the congregation turned their backs upon the minister in an involuntary way; of the Academy, built in 1830 of timber from the old cantonment barracks on Greenbush Heights—timber almost proof against cannon-shot; of the slaves in the old days before 1826, baptized and received into the fellowship of the church; of dear old "Sauer" Herrick, the dusky saint who always sat in the gallery at the minister's left as near as she could get, encouraging him by her constant presence, and helping him more than he knew by her humble faith—a saint translated fifty years ago to be a glittering black diamond in her Saviour's crown; of the first Sunday school away back, which some of you still remember, with John O. Lansing as superintendent and the whole of the second chapter of Matthew for the first lesson, and very likely one or two more for the next—there was no nonsense about those old superintendents—of the rude vehicles for church-going; how the young men, dressed in their best, whatever that was, went barefoot, carrying their shoes until they came in sight of *her* house; and men and women doing the same as they went to and from church. It was hard for the old Hollanders to be obliged to receive the Gospel in the English language. And what work they made with the new language, often getting out what they did not mean to say, as when one honest Dutchman who had fallen from the upper story of his barn to the floor, described it as a fall "sixteen feet in circumference!"

There is a pleasant and authentic old story to the purport that two prominent members of the congregation, widowers, were seized simultaneously with strong impulses to seek the hand in marriage of a beautiful woman, a sister of your fifth minister. The lady was at Ballston Spa, which, at that time, was the great summer resort, and both gentlemen set out at about the same time for the springs, each in the hope of outstripping his rival and winning the prize. It was in the old days before railroads, and their heavy carriages made slow progress. But the rivals—one a Frenchman and the other a Dutchman—were resolute and eager, and for hours the issue was doubtful. The Frenchman won the race and the bride, who proved to be a prize indeed, an ornament to the society of Greenbush, and a wife and mother of rare excellence.

Time would fail me to tell of how faithfully the officers of this church have cared for its property, and how when anything needed to be done they went at it and did it, and did it well. *"Si monumentum quæris, circumspice!"* And in the old times when they needed money they asked for it directly in straightforward collections and subscriptions— no fairs, no oyster suppers, New England suppers, tableaux, excursions or concerts even—but money direct. Will ye ever come back, ye good old days?

But when the sons of God came together, Satan came also among them. The fathers had often sore trials with the careless and worldly in the church, and sometimes with themselves. Intemperance was a crying evil, and many and many were the faithful admonitions and tender appeals to the erring. Their christian discipline was very effective, because administered in kindness, and without delay. The careless were entreated to be "more punctual in attendance upon the Word and Ordinances." A member was suspended for trafficking in milk on Sunday, which Classis had declared to be a "violation of sacred law, and a reproach to the christian church." They used plain words. Drunkenness in a professed christian they called "iniquity"—they did not throw all the blame on the rum-seller. Attending a dance was designated as a "crime," and the offender must give evidence of repentance and reformation, or lose standing in the church. When offences were grave and repeated, public confessions were required and admonitions given. A member gave out, many years ago, that he had discovered a gold mine on his farm, hoping thereby, as was believed, and as he virtually confessed, to dispose of his farm to advantage. The church gave effectual attention to the matter and strangled the thrifty scheme. A member of Consistory who had been sued at law for a bill which he had paid, filed in defence a bill against the plaintiff, *which had also been paid!* The plaintiff was non-suited, but the Consistory felt that this following of a bad example was inconsistent with the Gospel, however it might answer the civil law, and admonished the brother to "avoid the exercise of such a principle for the future."

In the year 1809 it was reported that a certain

member of the church had been "guilty of very immoral conduct in wounding and ill-treating his wife." It was immediately "Resolved unanimously, that the said —— be and he is hereby suspended as a member of this church until the Consistory have satisfactory evidence of his reformation."

A case of elopement of a member of this church nearly seventy years ago, occasioned a new sensation in this quiet community. The delinquent was also charged with intemperance. Upon report of the affair, an investigation was instituted, and strong evidence of the truth of the reports being given, it was "Resolved, that Mrs. —— be and hereby is suspended from church privileges until she gives evidence of reformation, repents of her crimes and makes reconciliation with her offended family and this offended church." The records are silent as to the final outcome of the case.

A member disciplined for intoxication in the days before pledges for abstinence were thought of, voluntarily offered to the church in token of his penitence an iron-clad pledge to abstain in the future from all intoxicants, including, with stronger drinks, beer, wine and cider.

A very prolonged investigation arose in the case of a young man preparing for the ministry, and who had received aid from the "Van Benschooten Fund" for educating ministers for the Reformed

Dutch Church. He was charged with carelessness as to his financial obligations in several particulars, and as he was desirous of connecting himself with the Presbyterian Church, the use of the aforesaid money in his preparation was at first regarded as evidence of bad faith. But upon a very thorough inquiry into all the circumstances he was acquitted of all wrong intent and honorably dismissed.

Time will not permit me to relate, even if that were possible, the work that has been done to plant and nourish this Banian tree and bring it to this hundredth birthday anniversary. The half is not told, and eternity alone can tell it. As I survey it, I am reminded of an old Greek patriot in the days of Athen's glory, who, when he had undertaken to describe the mighty structures and monuments of the classic city, exclaimed exultingly, ere he had half completed the recital: "All cannot even be mentioned; *the* Athens was builded by the gods and by the ancestral heroes."

Here for one hundred years has Christ been preached as the world's only Saviour, and hundreds have believed and been saved. Here multitudes have been consecrated to the Lord in baptism, and multitudes have sat down to the Lord's Supper who now drink new wine with Him in the Father's Kingdom. The blessed promise which attended the founding of this church has received a noble fulfillment. The wonderful power which attended the early ministries has been felt all through the century. Were you rescued from sin through more recent visitations of mercy? It was a result, in great part of the faithful labors—the divinely-approved work of Romeyn and Zabriskie and Marselus and Liddell and their co-laborers in the church, who plowed and planted and harvested so well. "The Lord our God be with us, as He was with our fathers."—I Kings, 8-57.

Dear, dear old Dutch Church! Church of my fathers, Church of the Reformation, Church of God, all hail! "The past at least is secure." Hundreds of the blood-besprinkled bands who went up through great tribulation have left us their high examples and await us yonder. I want you who are descended from such an ancestry to look forward indeed, but to keep alive these memories as well. "Honor thy father and thy mother," which is the first commandment with promise. This precious old grave-yard is God's acre, planted for immortality. Visit it often; there are voices there speaking always. There is more life there under the sod than in many a busy mart of worldly life. The Resurrection was born in a sepulcher, and life and immortality were there brought to light. Honor thy father and thy mother! In this newly-reconstructed church, on the threshold of a new century, let us pray that our Father in Heaven will make "all things new;" renewed hearts and new lives, new zeal and new sacrifices. Let every Sabbath be a high day indeed; bring your babes into the sanctuary, and give them to their Lord in baptism. Let the Sabbath school lack for nothing, and throng the place of prayer. When your prayers shall be answered, as they will be, and the Master sends you the missing prophet, let his hands be held up as never before; and then, as never before, shall his work bear fruit. You must suffer my words for they are born of pride and love and hope and faith. Here for a hundred years have the tribes come up—and my kindred always among them—to the worship of the great King. Some honored names in this lapse of years are dying out of the records; who will take their places? O ye children of such a parentage, who are neglecting the God of your fathers, do you know what you are doing? Who will crown this centennial service by giving to God the most acceptable offering—the offering of his heart? I know you feel you ought to; I almost feel that you will. For the last fifty days of searching for this history I have seemed to be so near the sainted dead that I have felt a spirit of hallowed communion. Shall I speak to them about you? Shall I tell them that a hundred years is enough? That the story of their faith and the memories they left you, have, by the grace of God, prevailed? The child now born here of God shall die a hundred years old—aye, in a deep and blessed sense is *born* a hundred years old—born in answer to that first prayer of Eilardus Westerlo, born in answer to the prayers of a hundred years!

NOTE.—The historian—Rev. J. F. Yates, A.M.—who with such painstaking, elaborated the foregoing address, is the son of the lamented Christopher Yates, whose family has been identified with the church from the very beginning. He entered the ministry of the Methodist Episcopal Church, being licensed in 1846 and ordained in 1850, and has passed his whole ministerial life in that denomination.

It was a good providence that he had the leisure in 1887 to compile the history of the first century, and the church and people owe him a debt of gratitude which can never be discharged. As a son of the church he has shown a just pride in her past, is interested in her welfare for the present, and hopes great things for her future.—(P. T. P.)

Three young men from the families of the congregation have entered the ministry of the Reformed Church, and these being present were called upon for ten-minute addresses.

Rev. Edward Lodewick spoke on "The Reformed Church in relation to other Churches," as follows:

Beloved in the Lord Jesus Christ:—It affords me very great pleasure to be present with you on this grand occasion, and to bring you my hearty greetings as one of the sons of this church; for I look upon this church as my spiritual mother. .

I owe my early religious impressions, first of all, to my beloved, pious mother, whom years ago we laid to rest in yonder cemetery; and next to her to this church, when under the ministry of that good and holy man, Dr. James R. Talmage, who has also gone to his reward. Here, when a child, I gave my heart to the Saviour, and resolved, God willing, to devote my life to the preaching of the glorious Gospel of Christ. Here I received my early religious training, was fed and nourished with spiritual food during the pastorates of Rev. P. Q. Wilson (who is with us to-day), and of the Rev. W. Anderson, the memory of whom is very precious to many of us.

As I recall the blessings which God has showered down upon me through this church and her faithful pastors, my heart overflows with gratitude; and I thank the great Head of the Church that I am permitted to be present at your centennial jubilee, and personally present to my aged spiritual mother my filial salutations. May grace, mercy and peace be

EDWARD LODEWICK.

multiplied unto this church from the Triune God, Father, Son and Holy Ghost.

I have been requested by your corresponding secretary to say a few words in reference to "The Reformed Church in its relation to other churches."

I.

In reference to our relation with other churches, it seems to me that the Reformed Church intends to maintain her identity. We as a church are proud of our history. We love our distinctive doctrines, we are strongly attached to our liturgical forms, and to our catechism and our confessions of faith. All these are heirlooms which have come down to us, through many generations, from the fathers and confessors and martyrs of our church. As a church, we consider these things far too precious to be cast away for nought. Hence, when the subject of organic union with the Presbyterian Church was considered at the last meeting of our General Synod, the voice of our church was heard saying, "We have nothing against the Presbyterian Church; she is a grand, good and noble church, our most honored and beloved sister. But the lines are fallen unto us in pleasant places; we will keep the goodly heritage which God has given us; we have an honored name in God's Zion, with which we do not wish to part; we have a noble work before us which we must do; we will preserve our identity and our individuality."

II.

While the Reformed Church evidently intends to maintain her identity, her relation to other evangelical churches is one of christian fellowship. Christian fellowship includes three things:

(*a*) Christian love or friendship. We believe the entire Church of Christ to be but one family. Paul speaks of the Church as one family, a part of which is in heaven and a part on earth—"Jesus Christ, of whom the whole family in heaven and earth is named." It is called the Family of God, the Brotherhood of Christ, the Household of Faith. All christians are children of the one Heavenly Father. As members of one family, we love one another. We are "knit together in love."

History shows that the Reformed Church manifests this christian love in her friendly relations with other churches. She has been the refuge of many persecuted christians—the Hugenots, Waldenses and Covenanters. She has extended to them her helping hand, her sympathy and her love.

(*b*) This fellowship includes communion with. We believe in "the communion of saints." All true christians of every name are members of the one family of God. All are partakers of the same spiritual blessings; all eat of the same spiritual bread and drink at the same spiritual fountain; all are washed in the same cleansing blood; all have the same love, faith and hope. We are all looking forward to the same eternal home and glory; all are joint heirs with Jesus Christ.

The Reformed Church holds towards other evangelical churches the relation of christian communion. They are children of the same Father with us, and with us receive the same blessings.

(c) Fellowship includes friendly and intimate association with. Our Reformed Church has been, and is, in friendly and intimate relations with other evangelical churches. Our Synod sends her fraternal greetings to sister churches, and in return receives their salutations. Ministers are frequently called from other denominations to minister in our churches, and from our churches to labor in other portions of God's vineyard. Our pastors exchange pulpits with the pastors of other evangelical churches. We dismiss members to other evangelical churches, "affectionately commending them to their christian fellowship and confidence." We also receive members into the communion of our churches, on presenting certificates of membership from sister churches. Every time the Lord's Supper is administered in our houses of worship, we invite those present from sister evangelical churches to come with us to the table of the Lord. We are in intimate relation with other evangelical churches. We say to our sister churches, "That ye also may have fellowship with us; and truly our fellowship is with the Father, and with his Son Jesus Christ."

III.

The relation of the Reformed Church to other churches is one of christian unity. We believe in the Holy Catholic Church. There is but one true church; one vine but many branches; one body of Christ but many members, still one church. "There is one body and one spirit, one Lord, one faith, one baptism, one God and Father of all, who is above all, and through all, and in you all." This unity includes unity of doctrine, unity of work, and unity of worship. The Reformed Church is one with other churches in her belief in the fundamental doctrines of the Word of God. With our sister churches, we believe all those doctrines embraced in "The Apostles' Creed." This unity of doctrine, however, leaves room for difference of opinion in reference to the non-fundamental doctrines. We find this difference of opinion existing among our own ministers and our own people. So we may differ in many non-essential things from our sister churches, yet we are one with them in our belief in the great fundamental doctrines of the Word.

We are one with them in work and worship. Formerly our foreign missionary work was carried on by organizations not connected with our church. At first by the "New York Missionary Society," and afterwards by the "American Board." We have engaged with other churches in "the work of home evangelization." We frequently unite with other churches in worship, lifting our hearts and voices with them in prayer, and putting forth united efforts for the conversion of souls, and for the advancement of the Kingdom of Christ. We are as another has said, "catholic and at the same time loyal, liberal to others and just to ourselves." The relation of the Reformed Church to other churches may be summed up in Christian Fellowship and Christian Unity.

The Church Militant is a mighty army, divided into many companies, but each company has its place in the ranks of the Lord's hosts. All are engaged in the same spiritual conflict with the powers of darkness; all are fighting with the same spiritual weapon—the Word of God, which is the sword of the Spirit; all are marching under the same standard—the blood-stained cross of the Redeemer; all are shouting the same battle-cry—Christ and victory; all are under the guidance of the same mighty Captain—Jesus Christ, the King of kings, and the Lord of hosts; all shall be brought safely to the one Church, triumphant in glory.

Note.—Edward Lodewick was born in this parish in 1846, graduated from our institutions at New Brunswick, N. J., and was licensed to preach by the Classis of Rensselaer in 1872. He has ministered to only two congregations—St. Johnsville, N. Y., from 1872 to 1875, and Park Ridge, N. J., since 1875.—(P. T. P.)

Rev. P. Theo. Pockman spoke on "The Reformed Church and Education" as follows:

Dear Friends:—It gives me great pleasure to be here and to speak upon the historical position of the Reformed Church on so important a subject as Education.

My being here is a gratification, for here it was my eyes first saw the light of day; here it was my mind first learned how to reason and judge; here it was my soul first caught a glimpse of the Saviour, Jesus Christ. There is no other place on earth like this to me. I love these hills; I love the old school house; I love this church.

There is also a fitness in my being here to represent the educational interests of our beloved church, coming as I do from New Brunswick, N. J., where, in the providence of God I have been called to labor, for there our educational institutions are

P. THEO. POCKMAN.

mainly located. In that city is situated the chief source of religious instruction for the denomination. That city is the Mecca of the Dutch Church, to which pilgrims go every year to renew their devotion, and kindle a new zeal for spiritual work.

It does not require much understanding to believe in Jesus Christ to the salvation of the soul, for the Scripture is so plain that even wayfaring men need not err in finding the way of holiness; but it does require a trained mind to give a faithful interpretation of all parts of the Word of God, and a knowledge of the Truth (which is distinct from inspiration) must one have to unfold revelation to the eternal glory of men. To this end our church has always demanded an educated ministry.

The policy of the Reformed Church in America has been to copy after her old mother in Holland, and place the church and school side by side—aye, more, to place the school *under the charge of* the church. This idea is well illustrated right here. The school house in the rear of this church stands upon the church property, and the room over the school room is the old Consistory room, and the pastors in earlier years always had a supervisory control over the school.

So eager was the mother church across the water to have her policy adopted in the New World, that she attempted at first to control matters over here, and insisted that students for the ministry should receive their education in Holland. Her sentiments in favor of an educated ministry were heartily endorsed, but her determination to have our young men cross the Atlantic, and, at the expense of time and great means, secure their ordination abroad, was strongly resisted. Only twelve of them underwent the ordeal in one hundred and twelve years (from 1658 to 1770).

The desire to educate our ministers in this country led to strife, and finally to an open rupture with the church in Holland. When King's College (now Columbia) was established, it was understood that the Dutch Church should have a chair of divinity in that institution, but for some reason it never did.

Overtures were received from New Haven to have a chair there, but these were not accepted. There was also a decided effort made to have a chair at Princeton, but prejudices were too strong against it.

It was, however, in connection with this movement that Dr. Livingston, our first professor of theology, expressed the wish that all churches of the Reformed faith might be united in one Grand National Body. He believed it practicable, and that it would ultimately be accomplished.

Queens College was founded in 1766 at New Brunswick, N. J. In 1776 the building was burned by the British. In 1790 it was rebuilt, and I presume it is this same edifice that still stands in Schureman street, used as a store-house for furniture.

April 27th, 1809, the corner-stone of the present main college building was laid by Rev. Ira Condict D.D., pastor of the First Reformed Church. In 1825 the name was changed to Rutgers College. At least two thousand students have been under her instruction from time to time, and about fifteen hundred have graduated, some of whom have become very distinguished men.

The college is thoroughly equipped in every department, with a high standard of scholarship and an earnest corps of christian professors. Her library contains twenty thousand volumes, and her grammar school is in a very flourishing condition. Three hundred and fifty of her graduates have entered the ministry of the Reformed Church, and seventy-five have become pastors of other churches.

Our Dutch ancestors—members of the Reformed Church—were chiefly instrumental also in founding Union College, at Schenectady, N. Y., in 1795. One hundred and fifty of her graduates have occupied the pulpits of our church.

In 1863 the church, realizing the necessity of giving educational facilities to those who were rapidly peopling the West, established Hope College,

[12]

with a partially endowed theological department, at Holland, Mich., and at least forty of her graduates have gone into the ministry.

These three colleges, and particularly Rutgers, have acted as feeders to our Theological Seminary, which has now entered upon its one hundred and fourth year of service for the Kingdom of Christ.

Ours is the oldest theological seminary in America, having already celebrated her centennial in 1884. At first there was quite a difference of opinion as to the location of the seminary. Those representing the northern section of the church wanted it at Schenectady, N. Y. Those of the middle and southern sections vascillated between New York City, Hackensack and New Brunswick, N. J. Finally the last-mentioned carried the day, and the meager department which at first required very little room, and for a long time struggled for existence, at last leaped forth a strong and powerful Institution, shedding her benediction upon thousands. From her as a fountain-head of purity a stream has gone forth in no way tainted with skepticism or infidelity; it is not a muddy stream, but clear as the living truth itself as it issued from lips which spake as they were moved by the Holy Ghost. Everywhere her sons teach a pure Gospel, and insist upon the faith once for all delivered unto the saints.

Eight hundred and seventy-five men, strong in faith and prayer, have gone out from her halls into every part of the globe to bless the homes and soothe the hearts of the children of men. Five hundred and forty of these are still living. There is no seminary in the country better qualified to train young men for the ministry. Her five professors, halls, and Sage library of forty thousand volumes, furnish everything necessary to make students full, ready, and exact preachers of the Word. She is worthy of your prayers, your gifts, your sons. You may judge her by her fruits. Is the Bible to be revised? Her professors are represented on the work. Is Arabic to be studied in connection with the Hebrew? Her youngest professor prepares the manual. Do you want a man to gather the largest flock of any under-shepherd living? T. DeWitt Talmage, a brother of one of the pastors of this church and a graduate from our school of the prophets, is the man. Does the Congregational Church want a professor? She selects our Dr. Hartranft. Do the blue Presbyterians want a gospel of white, shining love? They take our Holmes, and Berry, and Raymond, and Taylor, and Salisbury. Everywhere her students are sought after. There has been no "short cut" into the ministry. A long course of study has been demanded, and in so far as this has been understood by other churches, the fact of one being licensed to preach by our church, has been a guarantee of proficiency and acceptability. So determined is the church in this matter that we cannot think of giving permission even to natives of foreign lands to teach their ignorant and debased fellow-men of the new and living way without a special training. Because of our sturdy adherence to this principle, Dr. Chamberlain, our veteran missionary, is now on his way to India with over $50,000, to endow the *first* Theological Seminary in all that vast country. In this we rejoice not unwisely. The sons of the East must conquer their own land for Christ.

We all rejoice that the great timbers that were first used a hundred years ago to build the barracks on yonder hill (Greenbush Heights) to shield the *soldier*, were afterwards used, fifty years ago, to build the Academy across the street, to shield the *student*. So let us glory also in the fact that in other places where ignorance was once intrenched and men learned war, there a premium is now being put upon education and the sons of men are studying peace.

The sword of steel falls useless from a paralyzed hand when the sword of the Spirit is raised aloft; and to teach our students for the ministry how to wield this latter sword with *unrivalled power*, has always been the aim of the Reformed Church.

WM. FRED'K ANDERSON.

P. Theo. Pockman was educated for the ministry at New Brunswick, N. J., graduating from the Theological Seminary in 1878. He has served three congregations—Fairfield, N. J., from 1878 to 1880; Greenville, Jersey City, from 1881 to 1886; and the First Reformed Church of New Brunswick, N. J., since January 1st, 1887.

Rev. W. F. Anderson spoke on "The Reformed Church and Missions" somewhat as follows:

The Church founded by Christ is an army for conquest, a vine whose fruit is to hang over the wall, a tree springing from the least of seeds to overshadow and protect the earth. Little by little into the heart of the church comes the love of the Master, which was the love that loved the world. Here and there first went out individual sons into the heathen wildernesses. This border warfare with outlying heathendom is full of divine and startling incident. The biographies of the pioneers of the church are the inspirational chapters of her history. Joshua before Canaan, Paul before Europe. The man called of God, leading the church into some new province of the unconquered Canaan, makes the Gospel still apostolic and still adventurous and missionary. The day for these valiant knights has past; all the grand feudal kingdoms have swung open their gates to the trumpet notes of the kingdom. This work has immortalized such names as Talmage and Scudder and Verbeck. Among the tribes of denominationalism our own little church has planted her forces in three eastern nations. Arcot, India; Amoy, China; Yokohama, Japan, are centers of our foreign missionary history. We began early and have maintained every field upon the territory of the enemy.

What every confessor of christianity needs to realize is his partaking of a world-conquering faith; that he belongs to an army of the living God, which must subdue all Philistine forces until it makes a land of Canaan, a chosen land of the whole world.

By the end of the first century the Church had marched to Rome; in the fourth she had conquered the civilization that then was. After a thousand years of union with the uncivilized, medieval tribes, awakened and justified with the Word of God and by the Spirit, she arose in the fifteenth century for her advanced work. To-day she is upbuilding everywhere. The missionary spirit is strong upon her.

In the train wagon westward, in the ship eastward she goes, building her schools by the temples, and even yet mingling the blood of her sons in the mob violence of idolatry and hate. But by the power of the flags of christian nations, she is carrying the greater and mightier standards of the cross, which will hold back not only the ferocity of superstition, but give freedom from sin and the liberty of the children of God to the people sitting in darkness.

The day is not far distant when the earth shall have outgrown savagedom, when neither wild beast nor uncivilized man can be found. Heathenism will have become a past era—a dead empire, because the knowledge of God shall cover the earth as the waters the sea.

What unselfish living, what cheerful joy, what cosmopolitan spiritedness and awakened and love-tempered zeal this advance of the Church upon the masses in city and country and nations requires of us. How we should consecrate ourselves for a life of extending His kingdom, by recalling to-day what has been done for us.

Brethren, up from the past come the names and faces of those who have carried on this local church; there is here spread out before you a record of pastors and people, more sacred and more interesting than Israel's Book of Chronicles, and to-day the church, which taught us of Christ, received us in confession and accepted of our services, seems to us as only a factor of God raised up, born for our training and advantage in all goodness and truth. We can say of this church, she was our mother, and here as children she taught us of God.

Standing to-day, with all the memories tender and fresh which she holds coming back upon us, we once again hear the laughter and shout of our play days and see the beaming faces of boyhood and girlhood. Once again we are banded in that early life of work and of play, of confession, education and worship. There comes over us the tragic sweetness of the past goodness of God. "I will be a God to thee and to thy seed after thee."

The true godly spirit and christian fellowship of this local church is felt and acknowledged by all of us who were permitted to be joined to her. By all she has wrought for us, by all she has taught us, we will not but be true to her mission in us, passing down to others that which we have received from her. Fellow church members, fellow classmates and school mates, let us see to it that we possess the spirit of our common Master, who said, "After ye are converted, strengthen the brethren." "Go ye into all the world and preach the Gospel to every creature." Fast gathers the night upon us, in which no man can work. Speak, act, live the message of the Son of God, and when the still hour comes to us, we shall be carried to the high battlements, out from which even now are gazing the cloud of witnesses watching Christ's Church conquering the world.

Note.—W. Frederick Anderson, the son of Rev. William Anderson, graduated from Rutgers College in 1875, then taught one year in the Albany High School, after which he entered the Presbyterian Theological Seminary at Princeton, N. J., and finished his course in 1879. His first charge was in the Presbyterian Church at Chatham, N. J. When his father's health failed so that it was impossible for him to discharge his full duties, Frederick was called to be his father's associate in the pastorate at Fordham, where he continues his work, as sole pastor since his father's death, with ever-increasing efficiency and success.—(P. T. P.)

Greetings from neighboring ministers and friends succeeded these addresses.

LETTER FROM REV. IRA VAN ALLEN, OF WYNANTSKILL.

WYNANTSKILL, N. Y., Nov. 15, 1887.

To the Reformed Church at East Greenbush:

The grace of our Lord Jesus Christ be with you. The Reformed Protestant Dutch Church of Wynantskill sends greetings to her elder sister on the occasion of her centennial birthday, joining you in praising Almighty God for the blessings of the past, and praying for your continued and increased prosperity.

We are bound together by nearly twenty years of union under the same pastoral care.

I need not refer to the changes the passing years have wrought, nor recall names sacred to memory. In less than another decade we will stand where you do to-day, with one hundred years of history recorded, and the great untried future before us.

One by one the laborers are called to their reward and others take their places.

> Long on earth will men have place,
> Not much longer, I.

Those who now stand in our churches, in pulpit and in pew, "holding forth the word of life," must soon pass away, but thank God his church shall live while time shall be. Receive this our greeting in the name of Jesus Christ, who is "head over all things to the church, which is His body, the fullness of Him that filleth all in all."

IRA VAN ALLEN,
Pastor of the Reformed Protestant Dutch Church of Wynantskill.

LETTER FROM REV. D. K. VAN DOREN, OF MIDDLEBURGH, N. Y.

MIDDLEBURGH, N. Y., Nov. 16, 1887.

Mr. J. P. Van Ness:

DEAR SIR:—Permit me as an individual and as stated clerk of this Classis to extend my own greeting, and also that of the brethren of the Classis of Schoharie, to your venerable and strong church. But few of our country churches that have been established as long as that of East Greenbush have the numerical strength that it has. In this Classis we have several organizations that have been long established, but with the exception of two, they are in a very weak condition. Schoharie and Middleburgh churches, that are now over one hundred and fifty years of age, are by no means strong, yet these are the only ones of any vigor. Churches of other denominations have, since the organization of our churches, been built, and these have their share of attendants.

I trust East Greenbush will have a happy and successful centennial, at which she will be inspired with greater zeal and courage for future work. May she ever remain a shining light that shineth more and more, dispelling the moral darkness around her, and may new members flock unto the gates and fill her sacred courts on the holy Sabbath.

"Pray for the peace of Jerusalem. They shall prosper that love thee." Sincerely yours,

D. K. VAN DOREN,
Stated Clerk of the Classis of Schoharie.

PERSONAL GREETING BY REV. NORMAN F. NICKERSON.

DEAR CHRISTIAN BRETHREN AND FRIENDS :—I bring to you, on this occasion, the greetings of a sister church, in whose cemetery stands the pure, white marble shaft, which marks the spot where slumbers the dust of the brother of him whom you have so highly honored and eulogized this day, because he was the first and well-beloved pastor of your church. I refer to the Rev. Thomas Romeyn, of Glenville, N. Y., the grandson of whom, bearing the same name and residing in the same town, has been present at your festivities this day. There is also a great-grandson of the same name who, let us hope, may at some future period, become a minister like unto his great grandsire. In consideration of this relationship of the two churches, somehow I seem to feel like a second cousin to you myself.

Although in an unofficial capacity, I also present to you greeting from a sister Classis, small in territory, but by no means least in influence and historic incident, viz.: Schenectady, or the venerable Classis of Dort, the eldest daughter of Albany Classis.

At this late hour, I am fully conscious that I must avoid making a lengthy address lest I weary you beyond courteous endurance. I can therefore only rapidly mention a few topics which are suggested by this occasion, and which I must leave for yourselves to clothe with their proper environments. Let us first of all answer the inquiry—What, to us, is the meaning of this centennial?

1. It means the history of four generations of human existence, inclusive of those on the stage of life then (1787) and now (1887). It means a weight in souls, passed on from this lower house, up through the shining portals of the church invisible.

Estimating the number of "the redeemed" of this church, furnished to the heavenly gathering, at the very low estimate of two hundred and fifty per generation, you have well on to a regiment of one thousand veterans in that invisible host—quite a little army, if they can be looking down upon you to-day and participating in your thanksgiving, to help you in swelling the pæans of praise to Him, unto whom all the praise belongs. These all in their day and generation have fought the battle bravely for the redemption of the world from sin, even as you are doing now, and abandoned the weapons of their warfare only when mustered out of this church in order to join the regiment fast forming above.

It is a weight in influence, morally and politically. The numerical amount cannot be estimated of the influence for good, and the elevation of the moral and political purity which this church has exerted on the surrounding community during the past one hundred years.

It is pretty generally conceded that if all the churches which stand as bright, green oases in convenient places in this dry desert world of sin, were to be annihilated, civilization would soon again recede backward into barbarism. Your centennial sermonizer, this morning, drew a very thrilling picture, in which he made you to stand in the foreground, here before this pulpit, while your ancestry took their stand in the aisle behind you, and he startled us all by showing to us a savage forefather standing at yonder door. Well, I hesitate not to assert, that remove all evidence of the Gospel as taught in and evidenced by the very externals of our churches, and we may pass the line of our descendants down either of these other aisles until we find a barbarian again standing at the door, and the savage hand of the descending scale clasping the bony skeleton hand of the savage of the ascending scale. It might likely be a well-favored barbarian, for it is not likely that the race would ever again relegate itself back into skins for clothing and caves for dwellings. But it would be a barbarian, nevertheless, and a case all the more mortifying for the lingering signs of civilization.

2. It means to us ten decades of improvements. We have heard from the narrative of your historian about the externals of the primitive church and of its successive structures, until the present beautifully ornate edifice which speaks for itself.

But the *people* have grown, as well as the church, until *now* your Sunday school boys and girls are better Bible critics than were most of the men and women of that earlier period—aye, perhaps we ought not to exclude many of the ministry. (Here the speaker, by way of illustration, narrated an incident in which he was detected in an inaccuracy of statement by one of his Sunday school teachers, which gave considerable amusement to the audience).

Besides this, new sciences have been developed, which have proven of great advantage to us as a church. We still possess all of our forefathers' sources of knowledge, together with one hundred years of discoveries, such as no previous age experienced. The last two decades have been meteoric in startling revelations and useful discoveries.

Theology has also grown. Mark you, I said not religion. That is still of the same old sort—good enough for all. But theology has grown to recognize that the more nearly the church crowds to Christ's idea and definition, "pure religion and undefiled," &c., does she put forth branches ever green, with perennial spring of eternal bloom. More and more does she nowadays put the second of our Lord's commands into practice, in the hope of earning the plaudit. "Inasmuch as ye have done it unto the least of these, my brethren, ye have done it unto me."

And it is well. The sooner theology resolves itself into "Love thy neighbor as thyself," the sooner will the problem of the two great evils of the age—intemperance and the wage evil—be solved to the satisfaction of all.

What we need most is a greater and more intimate heart-beat with the beat of the great heart of Christ for the mass of suffering humanity. We must get down to the gutter-cast, and holding on to Christ's hand and reaching forth, grasping their hand, lift them up until we can place their hand in Christ's. As in the electric lights, there is all the power in, but no communication between, the dark dead wires until a slender thread of carbon is placed between the extremities, when lo! there is light and illumination. So has it pleased our Lord to place His Church as a carbon, which by connecting the fallen to Himself, shall convey to them the light and illumination of eternal glory.

3. This, then, is the most important of all that this centennial means to us, viz., that the work and growth before the Church of Christ for the oncoming century is humanitarian; that our fellow-creatures, of whatever grade of fallen virtue or lost imagery of God, are to be picked up out of the sloughs of despond, set on their feet and brought to the wicket gate on the way to the heavenly "Beulah Land." She is to work out the direction, "Prepare ye the way of the Lord, make His paths straight," by removing the obstacles which pride of caste has placed in the church's way of reaching sinners. She is delegated to pick up and renovate the sinners, themselves, and place them back on the way to welcome their and our Lord at His coming. We have too long forgotten what our Saviour said, "I came not to call the righteous but *sinners* unto repentance."

Then cometh the millenium! How to accomplish this work is now become the absorbing debate of the theologues of the various schools of christian learning and literature. I will close with the earnest prayer that you may prosper in the future, as in the past, and that in your own sphere you may do your talent's best work for the Master.

Congratulations were also offered by the Rev. Mr. Armstrong, of the Methodist Church in the village; by Rev. Mr. Luddon, of the Lutheran Church of East Schodack; and by the Rev. William H. Tracy, of the Third Reformed Church of Albany, N. Y.

The following poem, written for the occasion, was then read by Dr. Collier, the author not being present:

"A HUNDRED YEARS OF GROWTH."

BY REV. NORMAN PLASS.

From out his store-house took Jehovah God
   A precious seed, and with it earthward came,
Seeking a place, in all the world abroad,
   Where best that seed would magnify His name.
A spot he found, with worthless weeds o'ergrown,
   Barren of aught that yielded good to men;
'Twas there He bade the tiny seed be sown,
   And turned Him back to His abode again.
The seed was sown; the loving sons of God
   Gave it their constant and their tend'rest care;
And soon a tree with branches spread abroad,
   Budded and bloomed in radiant beauty there.

We celebrate to-day the hundredth year
   Since first that seed was thus divinely sown;
And as we come our hearts are filled with cheer
   To find that tree has all things else outgrown.
No more do worthless weeds infest the ground—
   Beneath that tree they quickly droop and fade:

Spreading its branches on all the region 'round,
  All useless growths have died beneath its shade.
It stands to-day upon this lofty hill
  Unswayed by all the adverse winds that blow,
So full of strength and sturdy vigor still,
  We scarce can doubt for centuries yet 'twill grow.

As children gather at the dear old home
  The gleeful tales of childhood's days to tell,
O'er field and woodland once again to roam,
  Beside the brook, within the quiet dell;
So here to-day within this sacred home,
  Endeared to every heart in divers ways,
The children of one family we come
  To live again the scenes of former days.
And though we have to manhood's stature grown,
  With Time's dull footprints furrowed on the brow,
We quite forget that many years have flown,
  And meet together e'en as children now.

But as we live anew those youthful years
  A thread of sadness runs through every heart,
And scarce can we refrain from bitter tears
  At thought of those whom God has bid depart.
By memory's hearth stands many a vacant chair
  Where now the loved forms no more appear;
They are not here these holy joys to share,
  They are not here these saddened hearts to cheer.
As we recall their ministries of love,
  We fain would have them share this gladsome scene;
But they are gone to that blest home above,
  There to partake of heavenly joys serene.

As veterans gather at the bugle-note
  From far and near, where'er they catch the sound,
Donning once more the soiled and tattered coat,
  Tenting again upon the old camp-ground,

So we, the warriors of the heavenly King,
  Gather upon this famous battle-field,
Those songs of triumph once again to sing
  Which to our valor have so oft appealed.
We build our camp-fires once again to-night,
  And gather 'round them as in days of old,
To feel their warmth, and by their flickering light
  Rehearse the stories of our warfare bold.

And as we tell those tales of by-gone days,
  Recalling scenes in which we fought and bled,
Our tongues can scarcely sound the words of praise
  Which they deserve who forth to victory *led*.
Those noble captains of our valiant host,
  Who faltered not when dangers hovered near,
Who fought the fiercest when the fight seemed lost,
  Who brooked defeat, and had no room for fear.
Would that they with us one and all might meet
  To join their voices in the victory song;
We'd cast our blazoned banners at their feet,
  And with their glorious praise the shout prolong.

As stand the stones along the world's highways,
  To mark the miles o'er which the travelers trod,
So these recurring anniversary days
  Point out the Progress of the Church of God.
We note the changes that have taken place
  Within these hundred years that now have flown—
The fashions old which we no more embrace,
  The forms of worship that have been outgrown.
Customs there were which are to memory dear,
  Hallowed observances, no more esteemed;
The children scorn the ways their sires revere,
  Neglecting rites which they most sacred deemed.

But we are not of those who blindly praise
  Those blissful days of old "when goodness reigned;"

We think that we have welcomed better days;
   Of all the customs have the best retained.
No more the long-faced look, the visage grim;
   No more the sermon, near an *endless* boon;
No more the tedious "lining" of the hymn;
   No more the doleful "pitching of the tune."
Such things as these do we no more regard;
   They came and went, living their little day;
We keep the kernel and the chaff discard,
   Retain the seed and throw the husk away.

Wand'ring one day beside a mountain stream,
   I watched it coursing down its valley bed,
Marking its gurgling waters' sparkling gleam
   Beneath the sun, as on its way it sped.
And as I watched I saw it linger long,
   With shallow course, where stooped the deer to drink;
And then I heard it blend its silvery song
   With that of birds which fluttered at its brink;
And now again I saw it stop outright
   Because of some obstruction to its course;
Then it resumed again its onward flight
   With greater augmentation of its force;

Amid it all pressing still boldly on,
   Running its rough and tortuous course along,
Winding this way and that, thither and yon,
   At every turn growing more swift and strong;
Until with quick repulse it sweeps aside
   All things that dare extend opposing hand,
Bearing them on with its increasing tide,
   Casting them high upon its gravelly strand;
Wearing its bed daily more broad and deep,
   Till on the solid rock its channels rest;
And then at length it sinks to silent sleep,
   From wandering free, upon old Ocean's breast.

How like to this, I thought, the Church of God,
  That stream that has its source on Sinai's height,
And thence flows on along this valley broad
  That leads beyond to realms of endless light.
Sometimes it moves with current smooth and slow,
  Its gracious blessings to dispense to all;
And then again its surging waters flow
  With speed of torrent swift or waterfall.
Sometimes its waters eddy 'round and 'round,
  Opposed by unbelief or doubts or fears;
And then again they start with sudden bound,
  Strong with accumulated force of years.

Wander with me along its rugged shore,
  And mark its course throughout the century past;
Note what obstructions it has triumphed o'er,
  Notice what driftwood on its banks is cast.
When men have tried to stop its onward course
  With barriers huge which have its current spanned,
It's swept them down with irresisted force,
  And strewed their shattered fragments on the strand.
It's hurled aside with sharp and sudden shock
  All heresies which have its course deterred,
Choosing its paths along the solid Rock,
  Shaping its shores by the eternal Word.

We note this Progress of God's holy church
  As it has onward run its arduous way.
Fruitless the task and more than vain the search
  To find a force which can its current stay.
We note the mighty volume it has gained—
  At sight of it our souls o'erfill with joy;
We lift our hearts to God with thanks unfeigned,
  And make His praises our sublime employ.

By Him its feeble course was first begun;
  By His own hand in all the way it's led;
Through all its devious paths its race is run
  To God the sea from God the Fountain-head.

And as when armies put their foes to rout,
  And on with loud huzzahs to triumph go,
Each soldier lifts his voice with lustiest shout,
  Because that triumph is his victory, too;
So we uplift our joyous shout of thanks
  Because God's Church is vanquishing all sin,
For we have place within the sacred ranks
  Of those who such a glorious victory win.
Whate'er the *universal* church has gained
  Within these hundred years so quickly gone,
Each *local* church has to the same attained,
  And in the conquest has rich laurels won.

We have to-day the leaves of history turned,
  And read what there is worthy deemed a place—
Those deeds of valor on their pages burned
  In characters which Time cannot efface.
We have recalled the desperate battles fought
  Upon this spot throughout the century past;
We've had displayed to us the laurels brought
  From various fields, and at this altar cast.
Here have brave warriors grasped the Spirit's sword,
  And with it put to flight satanic foes;
Here have they gained such victories for the Lord
  As on the *general* church a luster throws.

But what the need of tarrying here to-day,
  And thus renewing these five scores of years,
Unless from this review we turn away
  With loftier faith that shall becalm all fears;

Unless when Satan's fiendish hosts affright,
    And from the fight we're ready quick to run,
These deeds of daring shall anew incite,
    These noble victories shall then cheer us on.
Let us make sure the battle we begin
    Will for the cause of Christ advantage gain,
And then advance until at length we win
    The final triumph, and all foes are slain.

We sometimes gather 'round an aged tree,
    The seed of which was by a grandsire sown,
And there rejoice that it so sturdily
    Has upward grown for all that winds have blown;
We gather on the birthdays of a friend
    From year to year, the event to celebrate,
To him our heartiest wishes to extend,
    And on his blessings to congratulate;
'Tis thus we gather 'round this honored tree,
    Thus bid God-speed to this our sister-friend,
Wishing that many, many years may be
    Its happy lot, before its life shall end.

The Church of God—it shall unshaken stand
    As long as to the Truth it loyal proves;
Its healing branches shall o'erspread the land,
    And yield rich fruit to each who by it roves.
However hard opposing winds may blow,
    It shall resist unmoved their fiercest shock;
However strong the tempest-storms of woe,
    It shall remain enduring as a rock.
God sowed the seed, and God will it protect
    Until the final harvest-time shall come;
Then He will send his angels to collect
    Its ripened fruit, and come rejoicing home.

ADDITIONAL ITEMS.

The East Greenbush Methodist Church was organized December 2d, 1873, Rev. S. W. Clemens being the first pastor.

The chandelier and pulpit lamps at the Reformed Church were presented by Jacob Kimmey December 2d, 1872.

An organ was purchased for the Sabbath school August 16th, 1875.

On December 28th, 1880, it was determined that the church owned forty-two pews and that individuals owned sixty-four pews.

By action of Consistory of this date, *ten* pews were forfeited for non-payment of rent.

Steps were taken on December 18th, 1884, to have the cemetery incorporated.

On January 8th, 1886, Consistory gave a quit-claim deed to the cemetery association.

A piano was secured for prayer meetings and Sabbath school on August 3d, 1886.

The new matched-board *ceiling* was put on, the walls were papered, new window-curtains hung, a new sawed-pine shingle roof laid, and the interior of the church painted, during the summer of 1887. The carpenters were: Gilbert Westfall, contractor; Clark Waterbury, John Wright, DeWitt Reynolds.

The painters were: Frank M. Roth, contractor; John R. Payne, Alden Van Buren.

The *exterior* of the church has just peen painted (November, 1891), by Frank M. Roth, contractor. The color is Pompeian red.

SEXTONS.

The first person whose name appears on the records as *sexton* is Adam Cook, in the year 1806.

The following minute explains itself: "Joshua Cook is to officiate as sexton of the church, to heat the stove in winter, to open and close the church doors when there is service, and to provide *clean water* whenever children are baptized; and he is to have for those services the sum of three dollars, payable the one-half on the first day of February, and the remaining half on the first day of August in each year during the time he officiates. 1809, August 1st."

These persons have also served in that responsible position: Mr. Jessup, 1836; John O. Lansing, 1838; Isaac Dingman, 1841; J. H. Goodrich, 1846; Lorenzo Bedell, 1847; Harry Wilson, 1849; George Hulsapple, 1850; Hicks Hulsapple, 1853; W. C. Tourtellot, 1855; William H. Hulsapple, 1857; Reuben Van Buren, 1858; Barney Hoes, 1861; Joel R. Brown, 1867; David De Freest, 1872; A. D. Traver, 1877; Christian Vedder, 1881; William S. Miller, William Link.

TREASURERS.

As far as can be determined, these have performed the duties of treasurer: Peter Whitaker (or Whitbeck) 1801; Peter D. Van Dyck, 1802; Peter W. Witbeck, 1806; Stephen Hanson, 1809; L. Gansevoort, Jr., Cornelius Van Buren, James Lansing, Esq., 1823; John O. Lansing, 1833; Gov. M. Herrick, 1834; E. P. Stimson, 1838; Henry C. Lodewick, 1846; Jeremiah Hyser, 1847–50; Adam Dings, 1851–3; George Lansing, 1854–5; John N. Pockman, 1856–7; Heremiah Hyser, 1858–68; Jacob Kimmey, 1868–88; Edgar Miller, September 15th, 1888.

SUNDAY SCHOOL SUPERINTENDENTS.

The list is very imperfect: John O. Lansing, Elliot E. Brown, Henry Salisbury, Joseph S. Hare, Stephen Miller, William H. Rhoda, John R. Taylor, Sylvanus Finch, John DeWitt Shufelt.

THE ACADEMY.

The Greenbush and Schodack Academy was started and partly built during the ministry of the Rev. A. H. Dumont, probably in 1829. It was for a long time fostered and controlled by the church. Trustees were elected from the members of the church. Rev. Mr. Stimson is said to have taken a very active interest in the school, and was instrumental in securing a library. For many years it was a source of great benefit to the community.

Some of those who have been at the head of the institution, or have taught there, are these: Mr. Russell, probably the first principal; John Crum, about 1837; John Hall, 1838.

With Mr. Hall was associated, as classical teacher, Michael Hillard, an Irishman, said to have been educated as a priest; also James Hoyt, afterward a Presbyterian clergyman, who was his pupils' ideal of scholarship and manhood.

Rev. Samuel Hill taught somewhere about this time; also a Miss Anderson.

Rev. Peter S. Williamson had charge in 1843. In 1844, and for some time after, Henry Bulkley and his brother, Hiram Bulkley.

Messrs. Leach, Schimeal, William C. Hornfager and Fellows were identified with the institution at different times.

Between 1850 and '60 the Rev. William Waterbury was principal.

While the present district school house was being constructed (1835?) the school was transferred to the basement of the Academy and taught by a Mr. Graves, a venerable man.

During the war (1861-5) the building was used for hotel purposes.

About 1869 Rev. William Anderson opened a

boarding and day school, under the title of "The East Greenbush Collegiate Institute." From the outset it was a very flourishing school, commending itself to parents who desired a school for their sons and daughters where christian culture and refinement were taught, as well as the contents of books. Mr. Anderson's three daughters, Miss Darrow, Mr. Herman VanDerwart and others were teachers. In 1872 Mr. Anderson sold his interest in the Academy to the Rev. Isaac G. Ogden, a Presbyterian minister, who, with the assistance of Walter H. Ogden, his son, carried on a successful school for a few years. After this Charles Putnam Searle, now a lawyer in Boston, had a private school in the building for one or two winters. The Misses Steele were the last to use the Academy for school purposes.

DAWN OF THE SECOND CENTURY.

The last sacramental service for the centennial year was administered by Rev. Matthew N. Oliver, of Rosendale, Ulster county, N. Y., on December 4th, 1887, he supplying the pulpit on that Sabbath.

The first pastor of the second century is Rev. John Laubenheimer, who graduated from Rutgers College in 1883, and from the New Brunswick Theological Seminary in 1886.

He was ordained to the ministry and installed

JOHN LAUBENHEIMER.

pastor of the Reformed Church of West New Hempstead, Rockland county, N. Y., on October 5th, 1886. His call to this, his second pastorate, is dated October 31st, 1888. He accepted the call and began his labors December 1st of that year. The installation services were held on December 19th, 1888. For these three years he has successfully prosecuted his ministry among the people to their entire satisfaction, and now has every prospect of enlarged usefulness in the future. The present strength of the congregation is numerically one hundred and twenty families, with a professed membership of two hundred and twenty-five, and a Sabbath school of one hundred.

Long may the dear old church remain a beacon and a tower of strength to mortal man! Ever may she be blessed with the Holy Spirit's indwelling and power!

> "Long be our Fathers' temple ours,
> Woe to the hand by which it falls;
> A thousand spirits watch its towers,
> A cloud of angels guards its walls."

And now my task is done. The labor ceases. The pleasure and profit abide.—(P. T. P.)

PASTORS.

Jacobus Van Campen Romeyn, 1788–1799.
John Lansing Zabriskie, 1801–1811.
Isaac Labagh, 1811–1815.
Nicholas J. Marselus, 1815–1822.
Benjamin C. Taylor, 1822–1825.
Abraham Henry Dumont, 1826–1829.
John Augustus Liddell, 1830–1834.
Edward P. Stimson, 1834–1852.
James R. Talmage, 1852–1860.
Peter Quick Wilson, 1861–1866.
William Anderson, 1866–1876.
John Steele, 1877–1887.
John Laubenheimer, 1888.

FIRST CONSISTORY.
Elected Sept. 14, 1787.

Elders.	*Deacons.*
Abraham Ostrander,	Abraham Cooper,
Peter M. Van Buren,	John E. Lansingh,
Christopher Yates,	Casparus Witbeck.

1789.

Abraham Cooper,	Obadiah Lansingh,
Peter M. Van Buren,	Joh'n. Muller,
Christopher Yates,	Casparus Witbeck.

1790.

Consistory increased to four elders and four deacons.

Petrus Ham,	Jacob Schermerhorn,
Christopher Yates,	John E. Lansingh,
Barent C. Van Buren,	John Witbeck,
Abr'm. N. Ostrander,	Joh'n. Muller.

1791.

John E. Van Alen,	Barent Van De Bergh,
Abraham Cooper,	Obadiah Lansingh,
Christopher Yates,	John Lewis,
John E. Lansingh,	Johannis Muller,

1792.

Hubert Ostrander,	Thomas Mesick,
Barent C. Van Buren,	John Witbeck,
Steven Muller,	Jonathan Ostrander,
Petrus Ham,	Jacob Schermerhorn.

1793.

Jacob Schermerhorn,
John E. Van Alen,
Obadiah Lansingh,
Christopher Yates,

Jacob Van Alstine,
John Lewis,
H. K. Van Reusselaer,
Barent Van De Bergh.

1794.

John Witbeck,
Hubert Ostrander,
Joh's. Muller,
Steven Muller,

Nicholas Staats,
Thomas Mesick,
Harmen Van Hoesen,
Jonathan Ostrander.

1795.

Barent Van DeBergh,
Obadiah Lansingh,
John Lansingh,
Jacob Schermerhorn,

Cornelius Van Buren,
H. K. Van Reusselaer,
Gysbert Van De Bergh,
Jacob Van Alstyne.

1796.

Hendrik Shants,
John Lewis,
Hubert Ostrander,
Steven Muller,

Philip Staats,
Cornelius H. Van Buren,
Thomas Mesick,
Jonathan Ostrander.

1797.

Jacob Van Alstine,
Nicholas Staats,
Barent Van DeBergh,
John E. Lansingh,

William Witbeck,
John Ostrander,
Gysbert Van De Bergh,
Cornelius Van Buren.

1798.

Cornelius Van Buren,
Leonard Gansevoort, Jr.,
Hendrik Shants,
John Lewis,

Charles Smith,
Cornelius Dubois,
Philip Staats,
Cornelius H. Van Buren.

1799.

Obadiah Lansingh,
Gysbert Van De Bergh
Jacob Van Alstyne,
Nicholas Staats,

Peter Witbeck,
John Van De Bergh,
William Witbeck,
John Ostrander.

1800.

Obadiah Lansingh,
Cornelius Van Buren,
Gysbert Van Denbergh,
Leonard Gansevoort, Jr.,

Charles Smith,
Cornelius Du Bois,
John Van Denbergh,
Peter W. Witbeck.

1801.

Obadiah Lansingh,
Gysbert Van Denbergh,
Leonard Gansevoort, Jr.,
Cornelius Van Buren,

John Van Den Bergh,
Peter W. Witbeck,
Nicholas Van Rensselaer.
Tobias Van Buren.

1802.

John A. Ostrander,
Philip Staats,
Leonard Gansevoort, Jr.,
John I. Witbeck,

Peter D. Van Dyck,
Myndert Van Hoesen,
Nicholas Van Rensselaer,
Tobias Van Buren.

[14]

1803.

John I. Witbeck,
Nicholas Van Rensselaer,
Philip Staats,
John A. Ostrander,
Peter D. Van Dyck,
Abraham Witbeck,
David Seaman,
Martin Vin Hagen.

1804.

Philip Staats,
John I. Witbeck,
Peter D. Van Dyck,
Nicholas Van Rensselaer,
Abm. Witbeck,
Martin Vin Hagen,
Abm. Van Buren,
John M. Snook.

1805.

Cornelius Du Bois,
Philip Staats,
Peter W. Witbeck,
Leonard Gansevoort,
Abm. Witbeck,
John I. Ostrander,
Caper Ham,
Abraham Van Buren.

1806.

Peter W. Witbeck,
David Seamon
Cornelius Van Salisbury,
John Halenbeck,
John I. Ostrander.

1807.

Peter W. Witbeck,
John Witbeck,
David Seamon,
Cornelius Van Buren,
Cornelius Van Salisbury.
Richard Smith,
John Halenbeck,
Stephen Hanson.

1808.

Cornelius Van Buren,
Philip Staats,
John Witbeck,
William Witbeck,

Richard Smith,
Stephen Hansen,
Samuel Ehring,
Jonathan Witbeck.

1809.

Cornelius Van Buren,
Cornelius Du Bois,
William Witbeck,
Philip Staats,

Jonathan Witbeck,
Hubert Ostrander,
Samuel Ehring,
Evert Van Alen.

1810.

Leonard Gansevoort,
John Ostrander,
Cornelius Van Buren,
Cornelius Du Bois,

John Witbeck,
William Van Denbergh,
Hubert Ostrander,
Evert Van Alen.

1811.

Richard Smith,
John Miller,
John Ostrander,
Leonard Gansevoort,

Evert Van Alen,
William Fitch,
John Witbeck, Jr.,
William Van Denbergh.

1812.

John Miller,
Abraham Witbeck,
Richard Smith,
Philip Staats,

William Fitch,
Peter Ostrander,
Zachariah Link,
Wm. W. Van Den Berg.

1813.

Philip Staats,
Abraham Witbeck,
Leonard Gansevoort, Jr.,
John Tice Snoek,

Peter Ostrander,
Zachariah Link,
John Carner,
John Moll.

1814.

Evert Van Alen,
John A. Ostrander,
Nicholas Van Rensselaer,
John Tice Snook,

John Ham,
John Carner,
John Moll,
John P. Heyser.

1815.

Nicholas Van Rensselaer,
Richard Smith,
John A. Ostrander,
Zachariah Smith,

John Ham,
John P. Heyser,
Cornelius Van Salisbury,
Stephen Hansen.

1816.

Richard Smith,
John A. Ostrander,
Stephen Hauser,
Cornelius Debois,

Jacob Snyder,
John Ham,
John P. Heyser,
Cornelius Van Salisbury.

1817.

Philip Staats,
John Tice Snouk,
John A. Ostrander,
phen Hauser,

John Ham,
John P. Heyser,
William Fitch,
John Witbeck, Jr.

1818.

Abraham Van Buren,
John Halenbeck,
Philip Staats,
John Tice Snouk,

Peter Ostrander,
William Fitch,
Richard Miller,
John Witbeck, Jr.

1819.

Abraham Van Buren,
John Halenbeck,
Nicholas Van Rensselaer,
John P. Heyser,

Peter Ostrander,
Richard Miller,
Joseph Jessup,
Zach. Link.

1820.

Nicholas Van Rensselaer,
John P. Heyser,
John Ham,
Abraham Van Buren,

Joseph Jessup,
Zach. Link,
Casper Ham,
David Reghter.

1821.

John Ham,
Abraham Van Buren,
Stephen Hauser,
William Fitch,

Casper Ham,
David Reghter,
Henry Van Denbergh,
Andrew Van Buren.

1822.

Stephen Hanson,
William Fitch,
Joseph Jessup,
John T. Snouk,

Henry Van Denbergh,
Andrew Van Buren.
James Lansingh
William Hicks.

1823.

Joseph Jessup,
John T. Snook,
Richard Smith,
Peter Ostrander,

James Lansingh,
William Hicks,
John J. Miller, Jr.,
Martinus Lansingh.

1824.

Richard Smith,
Peter Ostrander,
John Hallenbake,
William Fitch,

John J. Miller, Jr.,
Martinus Lansingh,
William Hicks,
James Lansing.

1825.

William Fitch,
John Hallenbake,
John A. Ostrander,
John P. Heyser,

William Hicks,
James Lansing,
John J. Moll, Jr.,
Nathaniel Payne.

1826.

J. A. Ostrander,
Jno. P. Heyser,
J. J. Miller,
Wm. Fitch,

J. J. Moll,
— Van Denbergh,
N. C. Payne,
David Reghter.

1827.

Abrm. Van Buren,
J. Ham,
Wm. Fitch,
J. J. Miller,

A. Van Buren,
Jno. O. Lansing,
— Van Denbergh,
David Reghter.

1828.

John J. Moll,
Stephen Hanson,
Abrm. Van Buren,
J. Ham,

S. Nelson Herrick,
John Payne,
A. Van Buren,
Jno. O. Lansing.

1829.

Wm. Hicks,
Jno. J. Moll,
Peter Ostrander,
Stephen Hanson,

John O. Lansing,
Nath. S. Payne,
Jno. Payne,
S. N. Herrick.

1830.

John J. Hallenbake,
Wm. Fitch,
Wm. Hicks,
Peter Ostrander,

Henry Van Denbergh,
Stephen N. Herrick,
John O. Lansing,
Nath. S. Payne.

1831.

John A. Ostrander,
John J. Miller, Jr.,
John Hallenbeck,
Wm. Fitch,

Henry Van Denbergh,
Nathaniel S. Payne,
Stephen N. Herrick,
David Reghtor.

1832.

John P. Heyser,
John O. Lansing,
John A. Ostrander,
John J. Miller,

Harmon Van Buren,
John Link,
James Burton,
David Reghtor.

1833.

N. S. Payne,   Barrent Hoes,
S. N. Herrick,   James Burton,
John P. Heyser,   Harmon Van Buren,
John O. Lansing,   John Link.

1834.

William Fitch,   Governeur M. Herrick,
Henry Binck,   Jeremiah Heyser,
N. S. Payne,   Barrent Hoes,
John A. Ostrander,   James Burton.

1835.

Peter Ostrander,   Benj. Whitbeck,
Henry Van Denbergh,   Chas. Roda,
Wm. Fitch,   Jeremiah Heyser,
Henry Binck,   Governeur M. Herrick,

1836.

John Link,   Nicholas Slighter,
Henry Binck,   Barney Schermerhorn,
Peter Ostrander,   Benj. Whitbeck,
Henry Van Denbergh,   Chas. Roda.

1837.

Benj. Whitbeck,   David Harrington,
James Burton,   Joseph Hare,
John A. Ostrander,   Nicholas Slighter,
John Link,   Barney Schermerhorn,

1838.

John A. Ostrander,
Nathaniel S. Payne,
Benj. Whitbeck,
James Burton,

William Sprong,
Jeremiah Link,
David Harrington,
Joseph Hare.

1839.

John P. Heyser,
David Rector,
John A. Ostrander,
N. S. Payne,

David Harrington,
Joseph S. Hare,
William Sprong,
Jeremiah Link,

1840.

Adam Dings,
Peter Ostrander,
John P. Heyser,
David Rector,

Wm. Hulsapple,
Edward Elliot,
David Harrington,
Joseph S. Hare.

1841.

John P. Heyser,
Barney Schermerhorn,
Adam Dings,
Peter Ostrander,

Henry P. Barringer,
William Link,
Wm. Hulsapple,
Edward Elliot.

1842.

G. M. Herrick,
Henry Van Denbergh,
John P. Heyser,
Barney Schermerhorn,

Isaac Bink,
Cornelius Schermerhorn,
Henry P. Barringer,
William Link,

1843.

Henry P. Barringer,
Henry Bink,
G. M. Herrick,
Henry VanDenbergh,

John Van Sindren,
David N. Row,
Isaac Bink,
Cornelius Schermerhorn.

1844.

Joseph S. Hare,
Benj. Whitbeck,
Henry P. Barringer,
Henry Bink,

Garrett Lansingh,
David Defreest,
John Van Sinderen,
David N. Row.

1845.

Charles Rhoda,
John Van Sinderen,
Joseph S. Hare,
Benj. Witbeck,

Doct. F. B. Parmele,
Wm. Hulsapple,
Garrett Lansingh,
David Defreest.

1846.

Simeon Ostrander,
Barent Hoes,
Charles Rhoda,
John Van Sindren,

Garret Lansingh,
John Guftin,
Doct. F. B. Parmele,
Wm. Hulsapple.

1847.

Henry P. Barringer,
William Hulsapple,
Simeon Ostrander,
Barent Hoes,

William Link,
Isaac Bink,
Gerret Lansingh,
John Guftin.

1848.

Barent Hoes,
Wm. Sprong,
Henry P. Barringer,
Wm. Hulsapple,

Henry Salisbury,
Nich. Staats Rector,
William Link,
Isaac Bink.

1849.

Evert O. Lansingh,
Henry Bink,
Barent Hoes,
Wm. Sprong,

John N. Pockman,
Walter Ostrander,
Henry Salisbury,
N. Staats Rector.

1850.

Barent Hoes,
David Rector,
Evert O. Lansing,
Henry Bink,

Jacob Schermerhorn,
Elliot E. Brown,
John N. Pockman,
Walter Ostrander.

1851.

Evert O. Lansing,
N. S. Payne,
Barent Hoes,
David Rector,

Abram Ostrander,
Adam Dings,
Jacob C. Schermerhorn,
Elliot E. Brown.

1852.

Joseph S. Hare,
Benja. Whitbeck,
Evert O. Lansing,
N. S. Payne,

John Gilbert,
George Birch,
Abram Ostrander,
Adam Dings.

1853.

Simeon Ostrander,   Alpheus Birch,
Jeremiah Heyser,   Stephen Miller,
Joseph S. Hare,   Edward Elliot,
Benj. Whitbeck,   John Gilbert.

1854.

Walter Ostrander,   Geo. Lansing,
Barney Schermerhorn,   Christopher Yates,
Simeon Ostrander,   Alpheus Birch,
Jeremiah Heyser,   Edward Elliot.

1855.

David Rector,   William Elliot,
Charles Rhoda,   Leonard Rysdorph,
Abram Ostrander,   Geo. Lansing,
Barney Schermerhorn,   Christopher Yates.

1856.

Joseph S. Hare,   Henry Salisbury,
N. S. Payne,   John N. Pockman,
David Rector,   Elliot E. Brown,
Charles Rhoda,   Leonard Rysdorph.

1857.

Simeon Ostrander,   William Link.
Charles Rhoda,   John Gilbert,
Joseph S. Hare,   Henry Salsbury,
N. S. Payne,   John N. Pockman.

1858.

Jeremiah Heyser, Jacob Schermerhorn,
Adam Dings, John Palmateer,
David Defreest, Wm. Link,
Simeon Ostrander, John Gilbert.

1859.

Peter Palmateer, Edward Elliot,
David Defreest, Chancy S. Payne,
Jeremiah Heyser, Geo. Lansing,
Adam Dings, John Palmateer.

1860.

Simeon Ostrander, Geo. Lansing,
Joseph S. Hare, Stephen Huff,
Peter Palmateer, Edward Elliot,
David Defreest, Chancy S. Payne.

1861.

Simeon Ostrander, Geo. Lansing,
Joseph S. Hare, Stephen Huff,
Peter Palmateer, Edward Elliot,
David Defreest, Chancy S. Payne.

1862.

Jeremiah Heyser, John N. Pockman,
Adam Dings, Leonard Rysdorph,
Simeon Ostrander, Geo. Lansing,
Joseph S. Hare, Stephen Huff.

1863.

Joseph S. Hare,	Henry Salsbury,
Henry Bink,	Wm. Link,
Jeremiah Heyser,	John N. Pockman,
Adam Dings,	Leonard Rysdorph.

1864.

David Rector,	John Van Denbergh,
Elliot E. Brown,	Lewis Ostrander,
Joseph S. Hare,	Henry Salsbury,
Henry Bink,	William Link.

1865.

Henry Bink,	H. C. Lodewick,
William Link,	Reuben Van Buren,
Charles Rhoda,	John Van Denbergh,
Elliot E. Brown,	Lewis Ostrander.

1866.

Jacob C. Schermerhorn,	John Palmateer,
Leonard L. Rysdorph,	Stephen Huff,
Henry Bink,	H. C. Lodewick,
William Link,	Reuben Van Buren.

1867.

Jeremiah Hyser,	Wm. H. Rhoda,
Joseph S. Hare,	Zachariah H. Bink,
Jacob C. Schermerhorn,	John Palmateer,
Leonard L. Rysdorph,	Stephen Hoff.

1868.

John Van Denbergh,
Henry Salsbury,
Jeremiah Hyser,
Joseph S. Hare,

John N. Pockman,
N. Staats Rector,
Wm. H. Rhoda,
Z. H. Bink.

1869.

Adam Dings,
Wm. Sprong,
John VanDenbergh,
Henry Salsbury,

Jacob M. Cotton,
Stephen Miller,
John N. Pockman,
N. Staats Rector.

1870.

Henry C. Lodewick,
William Link,
Adam Dings,
Wm. Sprong,

James Seaman,
Andrew Tweedale,
Jacob M. Cotton,
Stephen Miller.

1871.

Edward Elliot,
Lewis Ostrander,
Henry C. Lodewick,
William Link,

Reuben Van Buren,
Isaac Hays,
James Seamon,
Andrew Tweedale.

1872.

L. L. Rysdorph,
Jacob Schermerhorn,
Edward Elliot,
Lewis Ostrander,

John Palmateer,
Martinus Lansing,
Reuben Van Buren,
Isaac Hays.

1873.

John Van Denbergh,
Joseph S. Hare,
L. L. Rysdorph,
Jacob Schermerhorn,

Michael Warner,
John Van Sindern,
John Palmateer,
Martinus Lansing.

1874.

Stephen Miller,
N. S. Rector,
John VanDenbergh,
Joseph S. Hare,

Wm. H. Bame,
Theodore Hover,
Michael Warner,
John VanSindern.

1875.

E. E. Brown,
Wm. Link, Senior,
Stephen Miller,
N. S. Rector,

Walter Elliot,
Theodore Van Decar,
Wm. H. Bame,
Theodore Hover.

1876.

Jacob M. Cotton,
Isaac Hays,
E. E. Brown,
Wm. Link, Sn.

Eugene Bame,
Eli Shaffer,
Walter Elliot,
Theodore Van Decar.

1877.

Henry Salsbury,
James Seamon,
Jacob M. Cotton,
Isaac Hays,

Wm. H. Rhoda,
Martin Streever,
Eugene Bame,
Eli Shaffer.

1878.

Stephen Miller,
Martinus Lansing,
Henry Salsbury,
James Seamon,

Michael Warner,
Frank Shaffer,
Wm. H. Rhoda,
Martin Streever.

1879.

John R. Taylor,
Stephen Hoff,
Stephen Miller,
Martinus Lansing,

John D. Shufelt,
Jacob Kimmey,
Michael Warner,
Frank Shaffer.

1880.

John Van Denbergh,
Andrew Tweedale,
John R. Taylor,
Stephen Hoff,

Reuben Van Buren,
Zachariah Bink,
John D. Shufelt,
Jacob Kimmey.

1881.

Joseph S. Hare,
Jacob M. Cotton,
John VanDenbergh,
Andrew Tweedale,

Cornelius Schermerhorn,
Wm. R. Defreest,
Reuben VanBuren,
Zachariah Bink.

1882.

James Seamon,
Isaac Hays,
Joseph S. Hare,
Jacob M. Cotton,

Wm. S. Miller,
Abram Palmateer,
Cornelius Schermerhorn,
Wm. Defreest.

[15]

1883.

Geo. W. Brockway,
John N. Pockman,
James Seamon,
Isaac Hays,

Sylvanus Finch,
James Elliot,
Wm. S. Miller,
Abram Palmateer.

1884.

Jacob Kimmey,
Wm. H. Rhoda,
Geo. W. Brockway,
John N. Pockman,

John A. Putman,
Jesse P. Van Ness,
Sylvanus Finch,
James Elliot.

1885.

Stephen Miller,
Zachariah Bink,
Jacob Kimmey,
Wm. H. Rhoda,

F. Albert Van Denbergh,
Theodore Hover,
John A. Putman,
Jesse P. Van Ness.

1886.

Jacob M. Cotton,
Jacob Schermerhorn,
Stephen Miller,
Zachariah Bink,

Thomas Black,
Michael Warner,
Albert VanDenbergh,
Theodore Hover.

1887.

Andrew Tweedale,
Wm. H. Rhoda,
Jacob M. Cotton,
Jacob Schermerhorn,

Alexander Traver,
John Moore,
Thomas Black,
Michael Warner.

1888.

John R. Taylor,
Isaac Hays,
Andrew Tweedale,
Wm. H. Rhoda,

John D. Shufelt,
Edgar Miller,
Alexander Traver,
John Moore.

1889.

James Seamon,
Stephen Miller,
John R. Taylor,
Isaac Hays,

Charles W. Burton,
Martin Streever,
John D. Shufelt,
Edgar Miller.

1890.

John Van Sindren,
Reuben VanBuren,
James Seamon,
Stephen Miller,

John Bame,
F. A. VanDenbergh,
Chas. W. Burton,
Martin Streever.

1891.

Theodore Hover,
Stephen Hoff,
John VanSindren,
Reuben VanBuren,

Jesse Brockway,
Wm. S. Miller,
John Bame,
F. A. Van Denbergh.

MEMBERS.

These persons were acknowledged as members at the organization of the Church of Greenbush:

1787.

Harman Van Hoesen, Yochem Staats, Peter Van Buren, Jonathan Witbeck, Barrant C. Van Buren, Benjamin Van Den Bergh, Christopher Yates and wife Catrina Lansing, Casparus Witbeck, John Lansing, Abraham Cooper, Jacob Ostrander, Gerrard Ostrander, Thomas Mesick and wife Maria Wiesner, Melchert Van der Pool, George Shordenbergh, Matthew Shordenbergh, Abraham Ostrander and wife Elizabeth Ostrander, Petrus Ham, John Miller and wife Catrina Herdick.

MEMBERS RECEIVED DURING THE MINISTRY OF REV. J. V. C. ROMEYN.

(Names followed by "c" were received on certificate.)

1789.

May 6.—Hubert Ostrander and wife Catrina Helm, Jonathan Ostrander, Evert Yates, Obadiah Cooper, Casparus Ham, John I. Ostrander, Jurrian Goes, Annatje Shans wife of Gerrit Van Den Berg, Maria Lansing wife of John E. Lansing, John Witbeck, Lyntje Miller wife of John Van Buren, Maria Ostrander, Obadiah Lansing, Jacob I. Schermerhorn, Catrina Brosee, c., widow of Hendrick Brosee, Catrina Mesig, c., wife of Stephen Miller, Thomas Mesick and wife Maria Wiesner, c.

September 17.—Abraham Van Den Berg, Catrina Shans wife of John Witbeck, Dinan, slave of Barrent Van Den Berg, Jin, slave of P. Ham.

December 20.—John Theis Snook, c., John Miller, c., and wife

Catrina Herdick, c., Catrina Moor, c., wife of Jer. Miller, Hilletje Van Den Berg widow of Cornelius Van Den Berg, Elizabeth Ostrander widow of Obadiah Cooper.

1790.

July 23.—Barrent Van Den Berg, Lena Van Buren, Elizabeth Staats widow of John Miller.

September 25.—Caty V. Renssalier wife of Cornelius Schermerhorn, Gertrug Vin Hagen wife of Myndert Van Hoesen, Catrina Freest wife of William Witbeck, Rachel Ostrander, Catrina Ostrander, Catrina Gnin wife of Leonard Witbeck, John Lewis and wife Maria Clarke.

1791.

April 21.—Stephen Miller, Widow Shibley, Johannis Witbeck, c., and wife Eva Waldron, c., Johannis E. Van Alen, c., and wife Nancy Friemont, c., Melchert Van Der Pool.

December.—Jesse De Foorest and wife Rebecca Van Zandt.

1792.

January 29.—Jurry Jac. Schordenbergh, c., Maria Michel, c., wife of Peter Ham, Herman Van Hoesen, c., and wife, Fryntje Witbeck, c., Annatje Staats, c., wife of Peter Van Dyck, Cornelia Van Alystyne, c., wife of Hendrick V. Renssalier, Annatje V. Schaick, c., wife of Abrm. Witbeck, Baatje V. Volkenbergh, c., wife of John Vin Hagen, Hendrick K. V. Renssalier and wife Alida Bradt, Nicholas Staats and wife Molley Salsbury, Philip Staats and wife Annatje V. Alstyne, Tiny Yates, Hester Emry, Fytje Miller wife of Herman Van Buren, Gerritje Smith, Elizabeth Smith, Hendrick Dekker and wife Catrina Fredenberg, Peter Van Buren, Tobias Van Buren and wife Jannetje Salsbury, Jacobus Vin Hagen, John Salsbury and wife Jinnetje Salsbury, Catrina Salsbury wife of William Agnew.

June 14.—Rebecca Waldron (widow), Guysbert Van De Berg and wife Jannatje Witbeck, John Bliss, Cornelia Lansing wife of Gerrit Yates, Cornelius Van Buren and wife Jannatje Van Der Pool, Johannis Van De Berg, Peter Goes and wife Annatje Van

Buren, Helmes Van Deusen, c., and wife Christina Kittel, c., Cornelius Du Bois, c.

October 4.—Eva Van Alstyne widow of Leonard Witbeck, Charles Smith, Daniel Hallenbake and wife Catrina Quackenboss, Hendrike Sharpe widow of Henry Hallenbake, Dorothea Hallenbake wife of Hendrick Van Buren.

October 7.—Marti C. Van Buren, Annatje Van Buren.

1793.

May.—Jacob Van Alstyne and wife Annatje Lansing, William Witbeck, Philip Duitscher and wife Elizabeth House, Phebe, slave of Peter Ham.

June 10.—Benjamin Bragge.

October 10.—Maria Amack, c., wife of John Hanson, Rachel Ostrander wife of Barrant Goewy, Maragrita Landt wife of Hendrik Ekker.

1794.

July 3.—Jeremiah Landt, c., and wife Maria Ham, c.

October.—Jellis Bat, c., Jannatje Cole, c., Jacob Hoffman, c., and wife Maragritta Rees, c., Cornelius Van Buren, Hendrik Shans, Harpert Widbeck, Gerrit Van Den Berg, Johannes Van Der Pool and wife Isabella Douglass, Jeremiah Shans, Nicholas Van Rensalier and wife Elitje Van Buren, Jacomine Bloomendall wife of Hendrik Crannel, Marie Goewy wife of Henry Ostrander, Gurtly Rees wife of Wm. Bartell, Rebecca Van Everen (widow), Sarah Van Everen wife of Jellis Bat, Rynier Van Alstyne, Peter De Freest and wife Petertie Van Alstyne, Cornelius Van Salsbury and wife Magtel Widbeck, Marti C. Van Buren, Abraham Van Buren and wife Neltje Van De Bergh, Rachel Freest wife of Matthew Van Alystyne, John Frison and wife Judike Van Buren, Jonathan Widbeck, Tobias Widbeck, John Hanson, Abraham Widbeck.

1795.

May 20.—Jacob De Freest and wife Anna Van Alstyne, Anna Ham, William Kilmer and wife Sarah Ostrander, William Lappius and wife Alida Van Dusen, Marretje Van Dusen, Jacobus Van Der Pool and wife Maria Muller, Jeremiah Miller, Gerrit Lyster, c., and wife Helena De Voort, c.

1796.

May 8.—David Seaman, Jacobus Salsbury, Martin Vin Hagen and wife Judith Carl, Peter Butler and wife Catrina Kilmer, Maake Him wife of Cornelius Van Buren, Abrm. V. Volkenbergh and wife Tennetje V. Volkenbergh.

1797.

May 8.—Leonard Gansevoort.

1798.

January 7.—John Staats Lansing and wife Elizabeth Cooper, Mary Van Renssalier, c., wife of Leonard Gansevoort.

1799.

September 28.—Catharine Miller, Jude, slave of N. Staats, John Vin Hagen, Conradt Ham, c., and wife Christina Stryd, c., and their daughter Catharina Ham, c., wife of Jonathan Dubois, Christina Ham c., and husband Nicholas Smith, c., Christopher Snyder, c., Jacob Snyder, c., Wilhelmus Snyder, c.

MEMBERS RECEIVED DURING THE MINISTRY OF REV. J. L. ZABRISKIE.

1801.

February 24.—Henry Hallenbake, John Hallenbake, Darley McCarty, Peter D. Van Dyck, Harriet Gansevoort, Catharine D. Gansevoort, Elizabeth R. Gansevoort, Anthony Sweazer, slave of Gerarchus Beekman.

1802.

October 24.—Nancy Haddock wife of Jacob Ostrander, Stephen Hanson and wife Rachel Thurston.

1803.

October 22.—John A. Ostrander, John Wilson, Letitia Smith.
October 23.—Nemer Aiken, c.

1804.

June 30.—John Carner and wife Jane Goewy, Peter Ostrander and wife Margaret Welsh.

1805.

June.—Richard Smith and wife Sophia Miller, Samuel Earing and wife Sarah Ostrander, John Pool.
November 2.—Charity Griffen wife of Cornelius Du Bois.

1806.

May 4.—Maria Van De Berg wife of Barrent Goes, Margaret Smith wife of Thomas Mesick.

1807.

October 31.—Caty Rush wife of J. T. Witbeck, Polly Curtis wife of Casper Ham, John Witbeck Jr.

1808.

April 30.—Elizabeth Du Bois, Tauike Witbeck wife of James Lansing, Elizabeth Lodowick wife of Smith Payne, Polly Rush wife of Albert Payne.

1809.

March.—Sophia Webster wife of John Witbeck Jr.
May 11.—Sally Link wife of Thomas Mesick, Ann Link, Catharine Link, Caty Mastin.
July 23.—William Haltzapple, c., and wife Susannah Link, c.
October 28.—Charity Traver wife of J. Mastin, Abiel Fitch wife of John Breese.

1810.

April 27.—William Fitch and wife Sarah Hanford.

1811.

May 1.—Eveline Gansevoort, Rachel D. Gansevoort.

MEMBERS RECEIVED AFTER THE DEPARTURE OF REV. J. L. ZABRISKIE AND DURING THE MINISTRY OF REV. ISAAC LABAGH AND UP TO THE MINISTRY OF REV. N. J. MARSELUS.

1811.

November.—Mrs. Miller, c. (widow), John Ham and wife Catharine Potts, Elsie Friar wife of James Smith, Catharine Yates wife of Dr. John Miller.

1812.

June 6.—Sylvanus Walker, Nellie Earing wife of David Goewy, Catharine Heaxt wife of John Manuion, John J. Moll and wife Gerritje Schermerhorn, Maria Ham wife of James Elliott, Sarah Burns wife of John O. Lansing, Cataline Schermerhorn wife of Gerrit O. Lansingh, Zacharias Schmidt, c., and wife Gertheay Holtzapple, c.

1813.

March 27.—Volkert Van Den Berg and wife Mary Vin Hagen.
October.—Margaret Campbell widow of Jas. McKown, Catharine Doty wife of Peter Johnson, Henry Smith, John A. Witbeck and wife Hannah Shuts, John P. Witbeck, Gertrude Bort wife of William P. Morrison.

1814.

April 10.—Hans Heyser, c.

The following persons were long recognized as members, but by some means their names were omitted from the old register and were not found in any of the Minutes of Consistory.—(Rev. Benjamin C. Taylor).

1808.

April.—Evert Van Alen and wife Deidrica Knickerbacker, Zechariah Link and wife —— Link, Polly Morehouse wife of

William Elliott, Henry Ostrander, John Miller. —— Heaxt wife of Stephen Miller, Hannah Ostrander.

MEMBERS RECEIVED DURING THE MINISTRY OF REV. N. J. MARSELUS.

1815.

November 3.—Anna Link wife of John Link, Cornelia Snyder wife of Nicholas Sluyter, Catharine Snyder wife of Teunis Snook.

1816.

May 3.—John Link, Hannah Holtzapple wife of Wm. Hix Jr.

December 7.—Margaret Hallenbake, Susannah Link wife of David N. Row, Sally Jessup wife of John Hayden, Elizabeth Card wife of Manassah Knowlton, Elizabeth Elliott wife of John Hallenbake, Nancy Bailey wife of Charles Doughty, Jane Teller wife of Rev. N. J. Marselus, Caty Van Buren wife of John Butler, Christina Bink wife of Jacob Snyder, Richard Miller, Eunice Hanford, c., wife of Joseph Jessup, Sarah Mynderse, c., wife of Samuel R. Campbell.

1817.

July 24.—William Staats, Henry Fradenberg and wife Tiny Potts, Catharine Philips, Maria Milham, Sarah Thompson, Mrs. Abia Scott, c.

1818.

January 30.—Gitty Hoes wife of Jehoicim N. Staats, Charity Witbeck, Hannah Lewis wife of Stephen Miller Esq., Catharine Rorapack wife of Barrant Van Den Berg, Cataline Keefin wife of J. McAlpin, Eleanor Williams wife of Andrew Van Den Berg. Getty V. D. Berg wife of William Staats, Eliza Drum wife of John Van Den Berg, Andrew Van Buren and wife Elizabeth Reghtor, Andrew Ham and wife Magdalen Ham, David Reghtor, Joseph Jessup Sn., Henry Philip, c., and wife Catharine Philip, c., William H. Philip, c., and wife Polly Philip, c., Elizabeth Smith, c., wife of Martin Krum.

August 7.—Barrant Van Den Bergh, Ann Staats wife of David Reghtor, Amy Bostick, Nancy Platt wife of John Herrick, Polly Sharpe wife of Evert O. Lansing, Catharine Lansing, Catharine Ostrander.

November 21.—Clarissa Burton wife of Nathaniel Payne.

November 29.—Elizabeth Payne wife of James Burton.

1819.

March 5.—Phebe Birce, Maria Pulver, Alida Schermerhorn, John D. Bovee, c.

September 24.—Hannah Milham wife of John Witbeck, Charity Acker.

1820.

April 28.—Henry Den Van Berg, Polly Lansing wife of John H. Van Rensselier, Abigal Allen wife of David Bell, Dorothy Weatherwax wife of James Philips.

August 10.—Judith Freezon, Betsy Smith wife of John D. Bovee, Caty Smith wife of Peter Smith, Tiny Mesick wife of Henry Van Den Berg, Catharine Miller, Elizabeth Ostrander, Ann Witbeck wife of Doctor Abm. Hogeboom, Eleanor Witbeck, Ann Lansing, Julia Fitch, Lydia Hulett wife of John G. Yates, Tiny Van Buren, Nancy Munroe wife of Daniel Doughty, Margaret Scott wife of J. Acker, Sally Du Bois wife of J. Palmer, James P. Powers, Stephen N. Herrick, Edmund Fitch, James H. Teller, Dorothy O. You wife of Jonathan Witbeck Jr., Lany Potts, Marshall Scott, Jane Eliza Lansingh, Barbary Van Alstyne, Polly Van Salsbury, Charlotte Delue, Maria Scott, Eliza Krum, Hannah Van Salsbury, Peggy Elliott, Catharine Decker wife of J. Mastin, Lydia Mastin wife of Benjamin Tallmage, Ann Degraw wife of William Hix (senior), Harriet Du Bois, Sally Van Voorhes wife of A. Du Bois, William L. Mastin, Jane Claw wife of Abram Van Buren, Ann Doughty, Sally Doughty, Mittina Campbell, Polly Reghtor wife of Peter Gardinier, Henry Acker, Charles Johnson.

November 24.—Olive Martin wife of J. T. Salsbury, Maria Ann Lansingh, Maria Lansingh, Mary Ann V. Renssalier, Rachel Witbeck wife of Isaac Knowlton, Polly Burton, wife of Tunis Smith, Alida Van Eps, Catharine Moor wife of David Ostrander, Ann Delue wife of S. Rorapack, Sarah Maria Wright, Louisa Amanda Wright, Maria Miller, Elizabeth Milham wife of Tobias Van Buren, Experience King wife of P. Kip, Caty Witbeck wife of John Pike, Maria Kip, Catharine Ham wife of Daniel Hallenbake, Nathaniel Payne, James Burton, Henry Witbeck, Martinus Lansingh, John Payne, William Hix, Joseph Jessup Jr., John Pike, John J. Miller Jr., James Lansingh.

1821.

May 11.—Governeur M. Herrick, Lydia Hicks wife of Cornelius Snook, Hannah Fuhr (Ford), Cornelia Salsbury, Maria Ostrander, Jerusha Treadway, c.

June 6.—Sally Hoghteling.

November 16.—Rasully Mastin.

November 18.—Lucy Maria Yale, Olive Eliza Yale wife of Doctor Goodrich, Maria Ham.

MEMBERS RECEIVED DURING THE MINISTRY OF REV. BENJAMIN C. TAYLOR.

1823.

February 14.—Martha Seaman widow of David Seaman.

March 5.—Anna Romeyn, c., wife of Rev. Benj. C. Taylor.

September 12.—Jane Van Dyne, c., wife of John Van Sinderen, Elizabeth Burwell (widow).

1824.

February 13.—Alida Moll wife of Cornelius J. Schermerhorn Jr., Andrew Van Den Berg.

August 13.—Annie Pulver, John O. Lansing, c.

November 4.—Sally Carpenter, c., wife of John A. Ostrander, Eitje Kittle, c., widow of John Van Den Berg, Taunche Goes, c., wife of Jehoiacim Gardinier, Charity Acker, c., wife of Daniel Smith, Christianna Bloomingdall, c.

1825.

February 25.—Awny Claw, c., wife of John Elkenbrecht.

MEMBERS RECEIVED DURING THE MINISTRY OF REV. ABRAHAM H. DUMONT.

1826.

December 3.—Flora, slave of J. A. Ostrander.

1828.

May 4.—Adam Dings, c., Eliza Winn wife of Abm. Pool.

1829.

January 25.—Jacob Ostrander, c., and wife Nancy Haddock, c.
September 4.—Geo. A. Huff, c., and wife Julia Ann Maston, c.

MEMBERS RECEIVED DURING THE MINISTRY OF REV. JOHN A. LIDDELL.

1830.

December 17.—Sarah Anne Yale wife of John Hall, Grizelly McGilpin wife of John Carman, Judah Fodder widow of Stephen Pool, Jane Vanbeuren wife of John Payne, Jane Vanbeuren widow of Tobias Vanbeuren, Cathrine Vanbeuren daughter of Harmon Vanbeuren, Henry Salisbury, Cathrine daughter of Henry Vanbeuren, Jeremiah Huyser, Mary Fodder wife of William Vanbenthuysen, Jane Martin, c., wife of Rev. John A. Liddell, Dinah Harrison, c., (colored).

1831.

April 1.—Jacob Dingman and wife Jane Vanbeuren, Ann Maria Schermerhorn, c., wife of Doctor John Van Alstyne.
July 1.—Margaret Showerman wife of William Lasher, Cathrine

Maria Vanbeuren, Christina Miller, Adam Dings Jr., Abrm. Pool, Dinah Anthony (colored), Sarah Banker (colored).

October 8. - Martha Semons, Eveline Gardineer, Alida Roribeck, Ann Maria Miller wife of Nicholas Miller, Emeline Salisbury, Jane Ann Ostrander, Polly Vanbeuren, Harriet Levina Bennet wife of Cornelius Vanbeuren, Ennis Vanbeuren wife of John Roribeck, Mary Vanbeuren widow of Garrit Vanderpool, Julia Loran Wright, Helen Cormick wife of Barrent Vanbeuren, Ann Ostrander wife of Joseph Hare, Maria Vanbeuren, Ann Hoes, Sally Maria Ostrander, Joseph Hare, John Roribeck, Barrent Hoes, Margt. Vanettin wife of Conrad Traver, Cathrine Vandenbergh wife of John J. Miller Jr., Cathrine Miller, Elizabeth Lowe widow of Jacob Staats, Ann Staats widow of David D. Semons, Sally Fox wife of Cristopher Yates, Maria Lasher, Mary Schermerhorn, Cathaline Schermerhorn widow of Garrit O. Lansing, Cathaline Lansing, Eliza Huff wife of Henry Ford, Christina Brooks wife of Casper Brooks, Hannah Miller wife of Jeremiah Huyser, Mary Divine widow of Joseph Hallet, Margt. Sheltiss wife of Lawrence Manzer, Conrad Traver, Benjamin Woodbeck, Susan Adam wife of Abrm. Baker (colored), Betsey Harrison (colored) wife of John Harrison, Eliza Lavender (colored), Hester Ryckman, c., wife of Richard Waring Esq., Elizabeth Carpenter wife of Barney Schermerhorn, Ann Miller widow of Arthur McClosky, Catherine Brees, Susan Woodworth, Eleanor Schermerhorn wife of Isaac M. Jessup, Barney Schermerhorn, Peter M. Vanderpool, John Pool—Junior.

December 30.—Emeline Mastin wife of Henry P. Barringer, Dorothy Pool, Nancy Fitch, Jane Porter wife of Benj. Woodbeck, Catherine Simons.

1832.

March 30.—Ann Shents, Jane Eliza Payne, Gertrude Schermerhorn, Sarah Ann Shibley wife of James Richardson, Margaret Woodbeck, James Ostrander, Mrs. Catherine Witbeck, o., wife of Jonathan Witbeck.

July 6.—Mary Staats, Ann Maria Pool, David N. Row, Cornelius I. Gardineer, Lawrence L. Manzer.

October 5.—Cornelius Hoes and wife Mrs. Sophia Hoes, Barrent Hoes Jr., Chs. Rhoda and wife, Mrs. Christina Rhoda, Nicholas Sluyter, Jeremiah Link, John Carman, Margaret Ann Vanbeuren, Sarah Ann Simons, Mary Fitch, William Sprong and wife, Mrs. Catherine Sprong, Jane Duryea Staats, Mrs. Jemime Jacques wife of Wart Jacques, Isaac M. Jessup, Sally Simpson (colored), Betsey Harrison (colored), Mrs. Ely Adams (colored), Margt. Burch, John Tuttle.

1833.

January 4.—Catherine Sprung wife of John C. Traver, Mary Williams wife of Chas. Doughty.

April 5.—Susanna Robertson wife of Christopher Sprong, Elizabeth Manzer, Charity Dubois, Catherine Vanbeuren, Willie Meesick, c., and wife Sally Ostrander, c., Andrew Oak McDowell, c., and wife Hannah Kitredge, c., Rachel Witbeck, c., wife of Isaac Knowlton, Eliza Brees, c., Mrs. Harriet Witbeck, c.

July 5.—Judy Lagrange, Christina Halsapple, c., widow of Philip Binck, Henry Binck, c., and wife Catharine Link, c., John Airhart, c., and wife Maria Kilmer, c., Evilina Airhart, c., Mary Ann McHay, c., wife of Benj. Mull.

1834.

January 5.—Harriet Wendall, c., Amy Stiver, c., wife of Jeremiah Becker.

MEMBERS RECEIVED DURING THE MINISTRY OF REV. E. P. STIMSON.

1835.

April 19.—Edward Elliott and wife Mrs. Mary Elliott, Miss Isabella Elliott, Miss Mary Ann Salsbury.

July 12.—Mr. Wm. Link, Mrs. Harriet Birch wife of Wm. Link, Mrs. Susan Traver wife of Jeremiah Link.

October 9.—David Deyo, c., Elizabeth Ostrander, c., wife of David Deyo.

1836.

January 17.—Timothy Newman and wife Anny Filkins, Cornelius Schermerhorn, Hannah Timson (colored).

April 3.—Mrs. Martha Taylor wife of Henry Genett, Thomas Mesick, David McLaurin.

July 3.—Mrs. Cornelia Tappan Genett widow of Dr. Hall, David Harrington and wife Susan Hulsapple, Abram Harrington Jr. and wife Getty Allendorph, John T. Snook.

October 2.—Sarah Adrian, c., wife of Rev. E. P. Stimson, Miss E. Rote, c., Adeline Harvey wife of David D. Semon.

1837.

May 7.—Sarah Ring wife of John G. Ring, Susan Stephenson, c., widow of Job Bink.

August 6.—James H. Mastin, c.

1838.

February 2.—John Coons.
February 4.—Sarah Mariah Traver.
May 4.—Margaret Traver, Sarah Bell.
November 11.—Eliza Dedrick wife of Z. Mesick.

1839.

February 3.—Teal W. Rockerfeller and wife Jane Von Voulkenburgh, William Hulsapple and wife Annie Snook, Isaac Bink and his wife Eliza Catherine Rockfellow, Eli Bois and his wife Eliza Christina, Elias Bois, c., Sally Ann Van Benthuysen wife of Saml. Earing.

May 5.—Henry P. Barringer, John Holland, Catharine Snook, Hannah Dings.

November 3.—Eliza Adrian, c., wife of Rev. P. S. Williamson, Jane Ostrander, c., widow of —— Westfall, Lucretia Dings wife of G. M. Herrick.

MEMBERS. 241

1840.

February 7.—Isaac Dingman.
November 13.—Catharine Milham, c.

1841.

May 15.—John Henry Yates.
August 8.—Harriet M. Yates.

1842.

February 6.—Mrs. Jane Goodrich.

May 1.—Garret Lansing, James H. Campbell, Elizabeth Campbell, Magdalene Grey, Hannah Eliza Snook wife of Wm. Semons, Mariah Ann Hulsapple, John Van Sindren, Loisa Shant wife of Garret Hulsapple, Sarah Ann Van Sindren, Deborah Payne, Elizabeth Payne, Hannah Eliza Hulsapple, Mary Ann Harrington, Dr. A. C. Getty, Caroline Siver wife of James Rosenkranse, Susannah Deyo, David Deyo c., and wife Elizabeth Ostrander, c.

July 29.—Mary Jane Hogan, Col. Broddum Yale.

November 6.—James H. Goodrich and wife Rebecca Ann Burton, Elizabeth C. Van Buren wife of Henry Palmer, David De Freest, c, and his wife Mariot Hilton, c.

1843.

February 1.—Phebe Eliza Huddleston wife of Wm. Philips.

May 14.—Dr. Parmelee, c., Mrs. Parmelee, c., Sarah M. Campbell, Sophia Clow wife of Daniel Sprong, Sally Rhoda, Susan M. Rhoda wife of Hermon Payne, Mary Mesick, Emma Hulsapple, Nathaniel Payne, David H. Hulsapple, Rachel Mesick, James E. F. Gage, Chauncey S. Payne.

August 6.—Leonard I. Rysdorph c., and wife Eleanor Earing, c., Sally Snook, Almira Snook.

November 5.—Stephen Van Rensselaer Goodrich, James Elliot, Mrs. Catherine Traver, c., Esther Traver, c.

1844.

August 4.—Albertim Schermerhorn; Emma Elizabeth Yates.

1845.

February 1.- Catherine Moulton wife of William Sprong, Benjamin Mull, Simeon Ostrander, c., Hannah Fellows, c., Harriet L. Ostrander, c., Rachel Fellows, c.

May 2.—Francis W. Payne c., and his wife Olive Ann Brockway, c.

August 1.—Jane C. Huddleston, c., wife of Richard Huddleston.

1846.

February 1.—John Guffin, c.

August 3.—Robt. Strain, Emily Chamberlain, c., wife of Fred. Birch.

1847.

February 6.—Anna Maria Rector.

April 4.—Margaret Elizabeth Rector wife of Silvester Fulton.

November 7.—Nicholas Staats Rector and wife, Maria B. Shufelt.

1848.

February 6.- Obadiah L. Yates, c.

April 30.—Dr. John S. Miller, Evert O. Lansing, Wm. Elliott, Jeremiah Miller, Abram Ostrander and wife Pauline Traver, Christopher G. Yates, Barrent J. Van Hoesen and wife Catherine Miller, Walter Ostrander and wife Eliza Ann Wilber, John Gilbert, Elliott E. Brown and wife Sally Jane Page, Jeremiah Leary (Roman Catholic), Jeremiah Hoff, George Hulsapple, Isaac K. Morrison and wife Laurietta Sprong, John M. Van DeCarr, Wm. Felix Hulsapple, Robt. Smith, Stephen I. Miller and his wife Christiana Lasher, John N. Pockman, George Lansing, Jacob C. Schermerhorn and wife Jane Kimme, George W. Birch and wife, Susan Caroline, Conrad Race, Edmund Cooper and wife Susannah Kemp, Orpha Torry wife of Jeremiah Miller, Margaret Hyser wife of L. P. Traver, Elizabeth Traver, Sophia A. Hyser, Sarah Defreest, Catherine Maria Hoff, Sarah

E. Haynor, Viletta Hulsapple, Mary Jane Hoes, Mary L. Knowlton, Harriet F. Stimson wife of N. Van Sindren, Sarah Ann Birch, Christina Ostrander wife of J. P. Ostrander, Cornelia Link wife of George D. Shibley.

August 6.—John Cotton. c., and wife Maria Bame, c.

1850.

March 2.—Julia Campbell, Peter Dings and wife Mary Coons.
September 1.—Almira Birch.
November 3.—Christopher Bartel.
December 1.—Adam Dings, c., Christina Rector, c., Alpheus Birch and wife Tynetta Newkirk.

1851.

December 21.—John Gilbert, c., and wife Jane Ostrander, c.

MEMBERS RECEIVED DURING THE MINISTRY OF REV. J. R. TALMAGE.

1852.

December 3.—Mary Shufelt, c., wife of Rev. J. R. Talmage, Catherine Talmage, c., Catherine Barner, c., wife of Wm. Beame, Mrs. Edwin Willis, c.
December 9.—Eliza Burrage.
December 10.—Elizabeth Hallenbeck.

1853.

March 5.—Hannah C. Hare, Leonard L. Rysdorph, c., and wife Sarah Maria Butts, c., Eliza Link wife of Barney Hoes.
June 6.—Catherine Ham, c., wife of Danl. Hallenbeck, Augusta M. Hallenbeck, c.
September 3.—Cathalina Lansing, Almira Ham, c., wife of Wm. B Tabor.
December 2.—Ann Stophilbeam, c., wife of Peter Stophilbeam, Tunchie Hoes, c., wife of Jehoikim Gardinier, Jane M. Jessup.

MEMBERS.

1854.

March 4.—Peter Palmatier and wife, c., Samuel Warren Cushing, John Palmatier, Margaret McGregor wife of Rich. Huddlestone, Elizabeth Caroline Ostrander.

June 2.—Lydia Hare.

November 30.—Ann Mesick, c., wife of Cornelius Hicks, Mrs. Dennis C. Crane, c., Harriet E. Crane, c., Mary Talmage.

1855.

March 2.—Andrew Van Dusen.

June 1.—Danl. W. Talcott and wife Viletta Hulsapple.

1856.

May 30.—Wm. Harvey Dings, Almira Phillips, c., wife of John Palmatier, Margaret Palmatier.

June 1.—Ann Staats, c., widow of Dowd D. Semon, Catherine Semon, c., Wm. Palmatier, Margaret S. Holt.

September 5.—Sarah Elizabeth Hare.

1857.

March 6.—John Walker, c., and wife Gitty Rosecrants, c., Frances Mary Sprung wife of Andrew Van Dusen, Electa M. Talmage.

1858.

March 5.—Mary Hulsapple, Lydia Hulsapple, Matha E. Schermerhorn, Sarah M. Slyter wife of Zech. Bink.

March 7.—Abram Palmateer, Zachariah H. Bink, John E. Hulsapple, Martha Ann Phillips.

May 28.—Stephen Hoff, Edward Lodewick, Mary Woodworth.

September 3.—Mary Ann Lansing, c., wife of Jacob Rector, Samuel Palmateer, c.

December 3.—Theresa Defreest, John Van Sinderen.

1859

June 6.—Sally Hyden, c., Cornelia Yates, c., wife of Jno. Van Denbergh.

MEMBERS RECEIVED DURING THE MINISTRY OF REV. P. Q. WILSON.

1860.

November 30.—Miss Isabella A. Hallenbeck.

1861.

May 31.—Mrs. Maria Cotton, c.
November 30.—Catherine Kimmy, c.

1862.

May 31.—John Vandenberg, Henry C. Lodewick, Louisa Clark.
September 6.—Elizabeth Burton, Jeremiah Link, c., and his wife, Mrs. Ann Link, c., Mrs. Stephen Miller, c.

1863.

February 28.—Mrs. Laura Woodworth, Reuben Van Beuren, c., and wife Sarah Rhoda, c., Garret Miller.
June 6.—Louisa Cotton wife of Cornelius Timeson, Miss Cornelia Schermerhorn, Mrs. David Moore.

1864.

February 19.—Betsy Blaney, Maria Manzer wife of John Proper, Hattie Matilda Proper wife of Saml. Palmateer, Emma Amanda Proper, Sarah Jane Buckman wife of John See, Mrs. E. Walker.
April 30.—Mrs. Rachel Mesick, c., Sarah C. Blaney, Mrs. May Palmateer, Mrs. Margaret Morrison.
August 6.—Mrs. Margaret Veeder, c., Miss Edith Veeder, c., Dr. Bower and wife Ameline Bower, Mrs. Charity Ann Miller, Mrs. Emeline B. New.

1865.

February 3.—Miss Mary Van Deusen, Mrs. Margaret Stumpt.
August 4.—Mrs. Mary Morey wife of Walter Elliott.
November 3.—Mrs. Caroline Hover wife of Lewis Hover, Mrs. Mary Barhyte wife of Albert H. Barhyte, Wm. Rhoda, Catherine Link wife of Abram Palmateer.

MEMBERS RECEIVED DURING THE MINISTRY OF REV. WILLIAM ANDERSON.

1867.

February 23.—Edward Green and wife Catherine Van Alstyne, William Frederick Anderson.

May 4.—Almira Lape, Eli Shaffer, c., and wife Sarah Terwillager, c., Mrs. Sarah Louisa Anderson, c., Cornelia Anderson, c.

August 4.—John Henry Lodewick, Harriet Louisa Anderson.

November 2.—Jane Lodewick, Harriet C. Bink, Andrew Tweedale.

1868.

February 1.—Jacob M. Cotton, James Seamon and wife Eliza Miller, Katie Seamon.

April 6.—David Moor.

May 9.—Benjamin E. Shaffer and wife Sarah S. Van Antwerp, Stephen Miller and wife Ann M. Keefe, Fanny C. Van Vechten, Hellen E. Phillips, Alonzo Sharp, Charlotte Kimbal widow of Albert H. Smith, Jane A. Schermerhorn, c.

October 31.—Albert Palmateer, Mary T. Van Vechten.

1869.

February 6.—Mary A. Schermerhorn, Magdalene V. R. Whitbeck wife of Edme Genet, Gertrude E. Whitbeck wife of Thomas S. Manley, Mary E. Muller, Peter Muller, c., Carolina Adolphnia Muller, c., wife of Robt. G. Maginniss.

May 15.—Libbie F. Schermerhorn, Mrs. A. Montania, c.

November 6.—Roseltha Kimball, David De Freest and wife Jane A. Kimball.

November 6.—Adelia Van Hoesen wife of Clarence Cotten.

1870.

February 4.—William Van Vliet, Theodore B. Van Decar, Philetus Theodore Pockman, Lydia E. Pockman, Mary Alida Van Buren, Sarah M. Van Buren.

MEMBERS. 247

February 9.—George M. Vandenberg and wife Jane H. Traver, Frank Albert Vandenberg, Martinus S. Lansing, Walter Elliot, Catherine J. Van Buren, Hattie L. Ostrander, Mary E. Mitchell, c., wife of John M. Link, Sarah M. B. Brockway, c., wife of Theodore B. Van Decar, Thomas Black, c.

April 30.—William S. Miller, Frank E. Shaffer, Harriet E. Rhoda, Mary C. Snook, Matilda J. Becker, c., wife of Jacob H. Snook.

August 6.—Theodore Hover and wife, Francis L. Cryne, Isaac Hays, c., and wife Catherine Van Akin, c.

November 6.—Jessie Lodewick, Margaret Goulder, c., wife of Isaac S. Lodewick, Louise M. Salisbury, c.

1871.

August 5.—Harriet Ella Smith.

1872.

February 3.—Lottie L. Walker wife of Lawrence V. V. Robins, Michael H. Warner, Elizabeth O. Wandell wife of Michael H. Warner, Rachel H. Robinson wife of Orris Clark, Florence D. Wakeman, Ida Louisa Taylor, Minnie Anderson, Hellen Slack, Carrie Mesick, Mary C. Barringer wife of Albert Warner, Matilda A. Clint, c., wife of Alonzo De Freest, Emma R. Van Buren, Ida V. Montania.

May 4.—William H. Bame, Eugene D. Bame and wife Christiana Hicks, Ida A. Bame, Eva M. Bame wife of Stephen H. Mesick, Mrs. Rev. I. G. Ogden, c., Walter H. Ogden, c., Florence E. Ogden, c., Rollo Ogden, c., Mary Elliot, c., wife of Stephen Hicks, Hannah Slingerland.

August 3.—Nancy Edick wife of Alexander Livingston, Permelia F. Livingston.

November 2.—Harriet Pitcher, c., wife of William Snook.

1873.

February 1.—Phebe T. Onderdonk, c., wife of David Onderdonk, Mary Onderdonk, c.

August 2.—Jacob Kimmey and wife Sarah Ann Koonley, Anna Jane Kimmey.

November 1.—Christina Hoes.

1874.

February 7.—John B. Vandenberg and wife Mary E. Forrester, Sarah Ann Vandenberg, Ewd. S. Vandenberg, John H. Bame and wife Mary E. Dings, Thomas G. Smith and wife Elizabeth Mason, Catherine M. Bame, Catherine Cryne wife of Richard Pockman, Catherine Rector, Genet S. Silvernail wife of Frederick Wood, Sarah Van Vaulkenberg wife of Abram Van Vaulkenberg, Alpheus Ostrander, Cornelia Hackney, c., wife of John Van Sindern, Augustus W. Kimball.

May 10.—Lewis Hover, Mary A. Walker, Margaret C. Lodewick, Catline C. Lodewick, Magdaline P. Ostrander, Mary A. Taylor, c.

August 1.—Julia A. Slyter wife of Andrew Phillips, Catherine Winnie wife of Jacob H. Slingerland, Orlando M. Hogle, George E. Anderson, Mary E. Bame, c.

October 31.—Charles A. Phillimore, Henry Bink, Mary Rhoda, Libbie B. Payne, Elizabeth C. Schermerhorn, Almeta O. Warner, Sarah Van Sindern, Ann Maria Hoes (widow), Alvina Van Deusen, c.

1875.

February 6.—John Van Slyk, Maria Van Slyk, Carrie A. Hover.

May 1.—Martin Strever and wife Dorcas A. Brockway.

July 31.—John R. Taylor, c.

November 6.—Nellie Van Vaulkenberg, Charlotte Douglass, c.

1876.

February 6.—William F. Link, John George Gerster, Margaret A. Cotton wife of William Hicks, Carrie D. Becker, c., wife of Wm. F. Link, Mrs. Henrietta Sherman.

June 3.—Hellen Van Sindern.

October 15.—Jennie Anderson.

1877.

May 12.—Willard Palmateer, John D. Schufeldt and wife Emma Cotton, Ella Sliter, c., wife of Frank Shaffer.

MEMBERS RECEIVED DURING THE MINISTRY OF REV. JOHN STEELE, D.D.

1877.

September 1.—Charles Van De Carr, c., James Elliott and wife Anna Schill, Martha Slingerland.

1878.

March 1.—Jacob Lansing Ostrander, Elizabeth W. Worth widow of John S. Van Den Berg, Anna Arrowsmith, c., wife of Rev. John Steele, Anna Steele, c., Louisa Steele, c.

June 9.—Henry Elliott, Mary E. Sweet wife of Henry Bink.

August 31.—Josephine Ostrom, c., wife of Wm. F. Shibley.

December 7.—Robert Taylor c., and wife Harriet Stalker, c., Clara S. Steele.

1879.

March 1.—George Henry Newman, James Weir, Jessie W. Schermerhorn, Clarissa Payne, c., Frances Lasher, c., wife of Jacob Gardener, George Henry Gardener, c., Cornelius Schermerhorn, c., and wife Sarah C. Myers, c.

June 1.—Lydia Salisbury wife of Christopher I. Lott.

September 6.—Mary Elizabeth Gardner wife of Francis Herrington, Maggie Van Slyke, Henry Taylor, Peter R. Hogle, Cattaline Van Voulkenberg, Elizabeth Shafer. c., wife of L. E. Gardner.

December 6.—Lydia Jessup, Jessie Benner.

1880.

March 6.—Anna Mary Tweedale, Emma Cornelia Rector wife of Oscar J. Lewis, Josephine Stumpf.

May 29.—Ann Burns, c., Ann Link, c. (widow), John A. Putman and wife Catherine Putman, c., Aaron H. Putman, c., Sarah Putman, c., William R. DeFreest, Mary Stumpf.

September 4.—Anthony Coon, Mrs. C. E. Garrison, c. (widow), Sylvanus Finch, c., Mrs. Sylvanus Finch, c., Wm. F. Finch, c.

December 4.—George Brockway, c., and wife Amanda Brockway, c., Mary Brockway, c., Emma Brockway, c., Walston Brockway, c., Jesse Brockway, c., Jesse P. Van Ness, c., and wife Ella A. Milham, c.

1881.

March 5.—Mary Ryerson Steele.
May 28.—Libbie Brocher.

1882.

March 3.—Margaret Niver, c., wife of Christian Veeder, Edith Veeder, c.

December 3.—Dr. Addison C. Roberts, c., and wife Maggie J. Cowan, c.

1883.

March 3.—Cyrus Lasher, c., and wife Ella Lasher, c., Eliza Moyer, c., wife of B. J. Walker, Willard D. Sprong and wife Paulina A. Melius, Miles Anderson and wife Mary A. Newman, Gilbert W. De Freest, George Van Buren, Charles Van Buren, George F. Warner, Elmer E. Finch, John Hauser, Alanson Hays, Charles H. Coons, Grace S. Warner, Jennie H. B. Snook, Anna L. Rhoda, Mary E. Moore, Sarah Schermerhorn, Esther Strever, Carrie E. Palmateer, Ida F. Van Buren, A. Kate Pockman.

June 2.—William E. Bame, Addie May Forepillar, John M. Mesick, Rosella Livingston, Matilda L. Livingston, Emma J. Edick, Alexander Traver and wife Charlotte E. Melius, John Moore and wife Cornelia C. Sliter, Elizabeth A. Phillips, c., wife of John M. Mesick.

September 1.—Elma Garrison wife of Aaron H. Putman.
December 1.—Jennie E. Rector, Jennie F. Herrington.

1884.

February 29.—Ida Jane Bell, Libbie Cack, David Henry Lape.

March 2.—Margaret Hymen wife of Peter Michael, Louisa Michael, Minnie Michael, Catharine Maria De Freest wife of John Clark, Emma D. Wands wife of Charles Earing, Jeanie M. Earing, Luella Sweet, Ida M. Crehan, Ella Crehan.

September 6.—Lydia Elliot widow of Leonard W. Rysdorph, Edgar Miller, M. Louise Caskey, c., wife of Edgar Miller.

1885.

February 28.—Vienna Weaver.
March 27.—Sarah A. Allen, c.
June 6.—P. W. Cramer, c., and wife Sarah A. Shufelt, c., Gertrude Shufelt, c.

1886.

March 6.—Samuel Germond and wife Maggie J. Lowrie.
December 5.—Maria De Freest widow of Emory Bouton.

MEMBERS RECEIVED BETWEEN THE MINISTRIES OF DR. STEELE AND REV. JOHN LAUBENHEIMER.

1887.

December 3.—Charles W. Burton, c., and wife Maggie Palmateer, c.

1888.

June 10.—John H. Van Sindern, Mrs. Margaret Black, Elizabeth Black, Alice Rhoda.

September 9.—Peter P. Burton, Mamie A. Van Sindern, August Byer and wife Adelia Newman, Lydia Coons.

MEMBERS RECEIVED DURING THE MINISTRY OF REV. JOHN LAUBENHEIMER.

1888.

December 15.—Jessie F. Randolph, c., wife of Rev. John Laubenheimer, Emma Laubenheimer, c., Abram L. Bame, Emma L. Bame, Jacob Rysedorph.

1889.

March 1.—Pamelia F. Livingston wife of Willard Palmateer, c.

June 1.—Georgia E. Johnson, Caroline Ackerman Sleight wife of W. H. Coons.

September 15.—Martha Cryne wife of Wm. Westfall, Mary Cryne widow of George Westfall, Minnie Carrie Hover, William Henry Coons, Frank Henderson Bell, Joseph Lewis Hover, Harriet E. Winnie, c., wife of Jos. L. Hover, Ora E. Knickerbocker wife of Irving Knickerbocker.

December 8.—John L. Miller, c., and wife Matilda Ostrander, c., Cornelia Gardner, c., wife of John E. Schermerhorn, Lucy Havens, c., wife of Frank Gardner.

1890.

March 9.—Mrs. Clara Carmen, c., Mary Frances Lansing wife of John Francis Miller, Frank Miller.

June 1.—J. I. Best, c., Mrs. J. I. Best, c., Rosa J. Hoff, c., wife of Jesse Brockway.

September 7.—John V. Davis, c., and wife Phebe E. Husted, c., Louis C. Stahlman, c., Mrs. L. C. Stahlman.

December 8.—Mrs. Susan Schermerhorn, c., Mary Lemire, c., wife of Alanson Hays.

1891.

February 28.—Louisa Cotton, c., widow of Cornelius Tymeson, Peter Ostrander, c., Minnie Comstock wife of Peter Ostrander, c., Carrie A. Ostrander, c.

May 31.—J. Allen Barringer, c., Mrs. J. Allen Barringer, Laura Sprague wife of Phillip Staats, Frank Newkirk.

December 6.—Mary B. Schermerhorn, Jennie E. Tweedale.

APPENDIX.

LIST OF ANTIQUITIES AT THE LOAN EXHIBITION,
DECEMBER 1, 1887.

Miss Berthia Staats—Dutch Bible, 250 years old.

Miss Martha Lodewick—Picture of the ship in which Rev. Ulpianus Van Sindern came from Holland in 1732, drawn by himself; white silk hand-embroidered wedding-dress brought from Holland, and worn by Mrs. Ulpianus Van Sindren in 1732; brass tea-kettle from Holland, 155 years; foot stove, 25 years; book published A. D. 1714.

Mrs. A. Tweedale—Pewter platter, 175 years; shoulder shawl, 100 years; linen table cloth, 100 years; Bible dictionary from Scotland; book, date 1777.

Mrs. James Lansing—Dutch Bible, 250 years; copper tea-kettle, 125 years; pair silver candlesticks; powder horn, 1756; large bowl, gravy dish and platter, 125 years; china plate, 125 years; bellows, 100 years.

Deforest Van Deusen—Pieced quilt, 70 years; housewife, 150 years; beaded purse, 60 years.

Yates' Family—Holland mirror, 150 years; Calvin's Institutes, 1611; Ulster County *Gazette*, January 4, 1800, in mourning for Gen. George Washington; $100 Confederate money; pewter plates and porringer, 150 years; an infant's dress, 70 years; picture of a lady over 100 years of age; linen towel, 106 years; child's rocking chair, 100 years; velvet work-bag, rose of Jericho.

Barney Hoes—American Preceptor, 1816; foot stove, 100 years; Holland mirror, set of chairs, 100 years.

Mrs. Walter Elliott—Bible, 1803; Doddridge's "Rise and Progress," 1744; hymn book, merino shawl, glass preserve dish, shoulder shawl, 85 years; tin bread tray, 100 years; china cup and saucer, 85 years; glass punch bowl and wine glass, 100 years; trunk, 100 years; foot stool, 107 years; soup plate, 84 years.

Mr. Jacob Snook—Jackknife carried in the Revolutionary War; potato hook, over 100 years; stable fork, 100 years; an augur, 100 years; iron chain obtained from soldiers, during the war of 1812, in exchange for milk; frying pan used before brick ovens or stoves were known.

Mrs. Jacob Snook—Two cups and saucers, 85 years; chair, 100 years.

Mary A. Schermerhorn—Chair brought from Holland, 1637.

Jesse P. Van Ness—Picture of Hon. Robert Monckton, major general, governor of New York and colonel of his Majesty's regiment, 1756; shoulder shawl, pitcher, tumbler and silver buckle, 1778.

Mrs. John N. Pockman—Book, 1821; knitting bag and sheath, 101 years; fancy work bag, 95 years.

John Van Denberg—Holland Bible, 1741; foot stove and andirons, 100 years.

Mrs. John Stumpf—German Bible, 1775.

Mrs. Mitchell Link—Small paper trunk.

John Van Sindern—Coat of arms, 1746; brasier brought from Holland, 1746; United States penny, 1783; petrified wood; New Testament and Psalms, 1715.

Mrs. Zachariah Binck — Striped coverlet, 150 years; stone crock and jug, copper tea-kettle and pewter dish, 100 years; scissors, 115 years; snuff box and snuff, 100 years; cup and saucer, 125 years; snuff box and bottle, 125 years; wallet, stamped 1776; pewter spoon and mould in which it was made, 150 years; sword of Revolutionary War, pocket knife.

Mrs. Wm. Link—Coverlet and linen sheet, 100 years; chair, 150 years; tea pot, plate, tea cup and saucer, 100 years; wine glass, 150 years.

Mrs. Stephen Miller—Cradle quilt, 80 years; brass candlesticks and snuffers, 80 years.

Wm. S. Miller—Mahogany cradle brought from Holland 100 years ago; coverlet woven in 1801.

www.ingramcontent.com/pod-product-compliance
Lightning Source LLC
Chambersburg PA
CBHW032059220426
43664CB00008B/1061